PETER ANDRE

MY WORLD

PETER ANDRE
My World
IN PICTURES AND WORDS

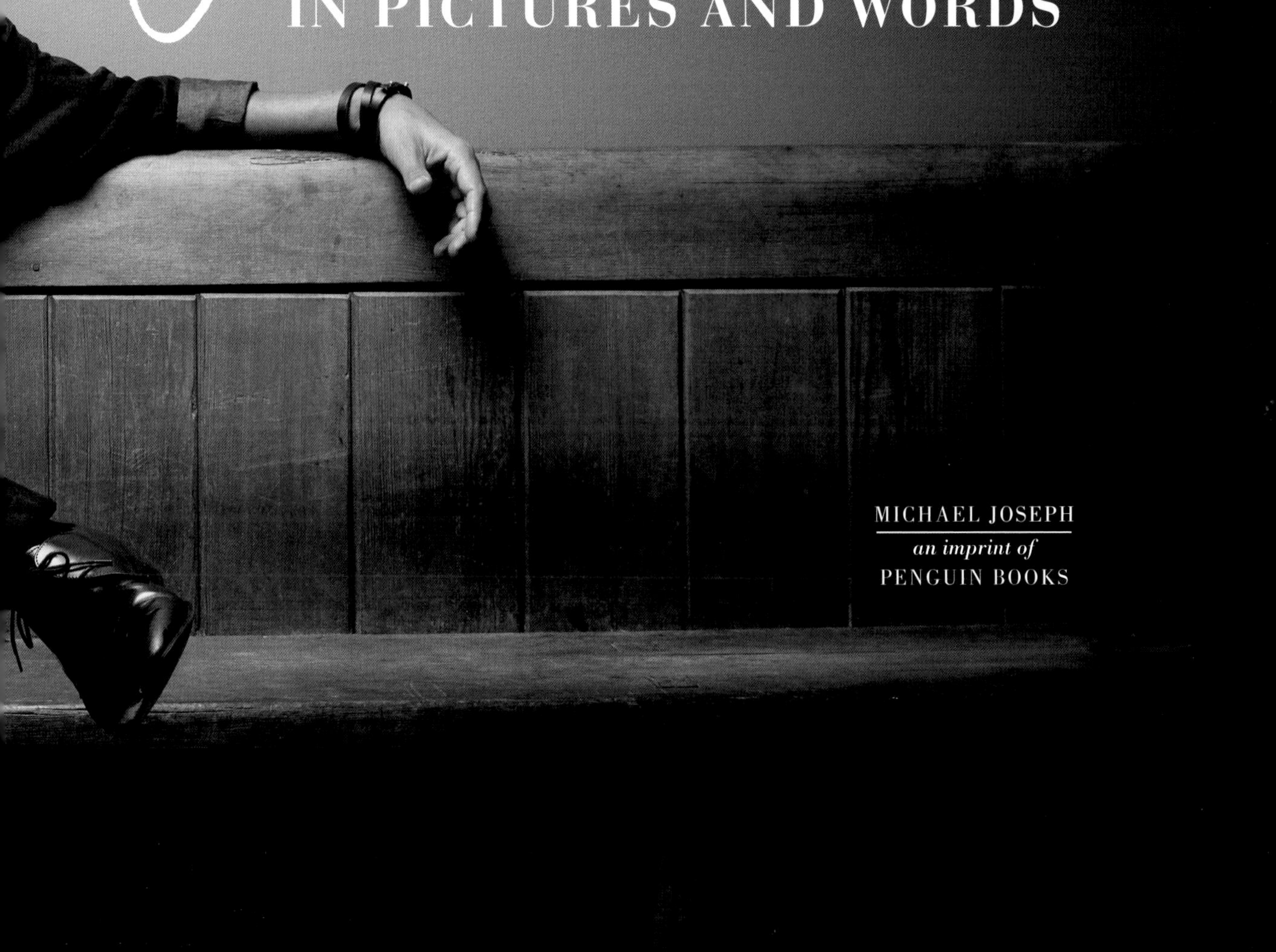

MICHAEL JOSEPH
an imprint of
PENGUIN BOOKS

FOR HARVEY, JUNIOR AND TIAAMII

MICHAEL JOSEPH

Published by the Penguin Group

Penguin Books Ltd, 80 Strand, London WC2R 0RL, England

Penguin Group (USA) Inc., 375 Hudson Street, New York, New York 10014, USA

Penguin Group (Canada), 90 Eglinton Avenue East, Suite 700, Toronto, Ontario,
Canada M4P 2Y3 (a division of Pearson Penguin Canada Inc.)

Penguin Ireland, 25 St Stephen's Green, Dublin 2, Ireland (a division of Penguin Books Ltd)

Penguin Group (Australia), 250 Camberwell Road, Camberwell, Victoria 3124, Australia
(a division of Pearson Australia Group Pty Ltd)

Penguin Books India Pvt Ltd, 11 Community Centre, Panchsheel Park, New Delhi – 110 017, India

Penguin Group (NZ), 67 Apollo Drive, Rosedale, North Shore 0632, New Zealand
(a division of Pearson New Zealand Ltd)

Penguin Books (South Africa) (Pty) Ltd, 24 Sturdee Avenue, Rosebank, Johannesburg 2196, South Africa

Penguin Books Ltd, Registered Offices: 80 Strand, London WC2R 0RL, England

www.penguin.com

Published in 2010
1

Copyright © Peter Andre, 2010

Photography copyright © Can Associates Ltd, 2010
With thanks to Dan Kennedy, Richard McLaren and Andy Neal

Additional photographs supplied by Can Associates Television Limited,
copyright © Can Associates Television Limited 2010

Additional photographs supplied by Peter Andre, copyright © Peter Andre, 2010

Additional photographs supplied by Gerard Farrell, copyright © Gerard Farrell, 2010

Additional photographs supplied by expresspictures.com, copyright © expresspictures.com, 2010

Additional photographs on pages: 21, 39, 44, 57, 72-73, 79, 80, 82-83, 84, 86-87, 89, 91, 103, 110,
119, 163, 165, 185 & 216 supplied by Rex, copyright © Rex, 2010

Additional photographs on pages: 5, 33, 171, 174, 175, 186, 187, 192, 193, 205, 206 & 228
supplied by Matrix, copyright © Matrix, 2010

Additional photographs on page: 69 supplied by Mirrorpix, copyright © Mirrorpix, 2010

Additional photographs on page: 61 supplied by Getty, copyright © Getty, 2010

Additional photographs on pages: 2-3 & 247 supplied by NI Syndication, copyright Fabulous Magazine -
News of the World / www.nisyndication.com <http://www.nisyndication.com> Photographer: Hamish Brown

Illustrations supplied by iStock, copyright © iStock, 2010

Tour posters supplied by Media Junction, copyright © Media Junction, 2010

'Distance' © Copyright Control/Verses of Style Publishing & Notting Hill Music/Jess Jackson Publishing
'Call The Doctor' © Copyright Control
'Go Back' © Copyright Control/Verses of Style Publishing & Notting Hill Music/Middens Music

The moral right of the author has been asserted

All rights reserved

Printed and bound by Firmengruppe APPL, aprinta druck, Wemding, Germany
Colour reproduction by Altaimage

Set in Bodoni, Engravers Gothic BT and Din

A CIP catalogue record for this book is available from the British Library

ISBN: 978–0–718–15694–7

Mixed Sources
Product group from well-managed
forests and other controlled sources
www.fsc.org Cert no. SA-COC-1592
© 1996 Forest Stewardship Council

FSC

Penguin Books is committed to a sustainable future
for our business, our readers and our planet.
The book in your hands is made from paper
certified by the Forest Stewardship Council.

CONTENTS

FOREWORD

When I sit down and think about it, my life has been a bit mad. Who'd have thought that little Peter James Andrea from Harrow would be where I'm at today? You couldn't make it up, even with my vivid imagination. To quote a song I'd rather forget, it's insania!

There's no denying that the past few years in particular have been tempestuous, to say the least – a rollercoaster ride, both physically and emotionally. I've got married, had children, got divorced and started to write music again. I'm still trying to get my head around it all.

Being a typical Pisces, I am very emotional and when I think of the journey I've been on to reach this point in my life it can bring tears to my eyes. Pisces are dreamers but we believe we can make it happen, we believe that everything is possible. I knew, when everything fell apart last year, that things would get better; experience has taught me that. I'm in a good place now and, despite daily tests, finally coming out the other side. Each day life genuinely gets easier for me. My father Savva once said to me, 'Never make the same mistake twice – make new ones.' Suffice to say I have learned my lessons the hard way, so I will try not to make the same mistakes again. My children are my priority, my life – I can honestly say that without them things would have been very different. It wasn't their choice to be brought into this world and they shouldn't have to suffer. They have kept me going and kept me strong.

My music is also very important to me. I have never been taken seriously, and up until *Revelation* I think people saw my music as a bit of a joke (okay critics, save your comments!), but I hope that slowly but surely I will change those opinions. I hope that the massive amount of time, effort and my own money that I've put into this is beginning to pay off.

I am a very positive person and I have loads of amazing memories of the past. I am a glass-half-full kind of guy and I always look on the bright side. Life is one hell of an experience – some bits are good, some bad, but I'm learning as I go along.

This book isn't an autobiography. It's something a bit different. It's a chance for me to let you into my life, and show you things through my eyes, to share with you the things that matter to me – family, love, music and so much more – the stuff that makes me me.

Welcome to my world . . .

WHAT MADE ME ME

WHEN I LOOK BACK ON MY LIFE, ONE THING I REALIZE IS THAT I'VE ALWAYS BEEN ON THE MOVE. SOMETIMES I'VE MOVED TO NEW PLACES TO START OVER AGAIN, TO HAVE A CHANCE AT NEW BEGINNINGS; SOMETIMES I'VE MOVED TO ESCAPE FROM WHAT'S BEEN GOING ON IN MY LIFE, OR EVEN, WITHOUT REALIZING IT, TO ESCAPE FROM MYSELF.

Nowadays, I couldn't be more settled. I've got a home in Brighton, and friends and family around me. The thing that keeps me here now is my kids. I might have left if it weren't for them – when you have kids, you realize that running away isn't always the best thing to do. You deal with it. I've had to learn to do that though, because right from a very young age, keeping on the move seemed to be a way of coping with the world around you. It was something my family started when I was just six years old.

A lot of people think I'm an Aussie, and it's true I spent most of my childhood there. It's also where my music career properly began. But I'm a Brit through and through, and my earliest memories are of England. Playing in the street outside our house, looking for conkers up on Sudbury Hill . . . I still remember seeing snow for the first time. My parents were staying with friends and had left us with a video of *E.T.* to watch, but minutes after we pressed 'play' the snow started to fall. We soon abandoned the film and were out throwing snowballs at one another.

WITH MY FAMILY OUTSIDE OUR HOUSE IN
SUDBURY COURT ROAD, JUST BEFORE
WE MOVED TO AUSTRALIA. CHECK ME
OUT IN THE CHEQUERED SHIRT!

IN HARROW ON MY BROTHER
CHRIS'S SHOULDERS — I'M FIVE
YEARS OLD IN THAT PICTURE.

We lived in Harrow, on the outskirts of London, in a place that wasn't just a house, but a home. We had happy times there (take a look at the picture of us all standing outside just before we left for Australia). It was pretty big but there were so many of us that it still meant that Michael, Danny and I had to share a room. I remember that my bed always had to be touching Michael's bed because I was scared of the dark. We were like Arnold and Willis from *Diff'rent Strokes* – I was Arnold and he was Willis. I looked up to him and wanted to be like him, and we have remained so close ever since. There was always something going on, thanks to the fact there were so many of us. I have four older brothers and one sister, Debbie, who is the closest in age to me at thirty-eight. My mum, Thea, and my dad, Savva, were desperate for a girl after so many boys, so when they had Debbie they were over the moon, the family was complete . . . well, until I put in an appearance!

Sudbury Court Road was next to a really busy street just behind us, but our road couldn't have been more different – it was peaceful, quiet, and – the best thing about it – it had a real community. It was multicultural, with Pakistani neighbours on one side, Jewish, Spanish, Italian, Jamaican and British families all rubbing together. It had a lovely feel to it – we'd take Greek dishes round to our Pakistani friends and they'd bring curries around to us: it felt protected, close and friendly. The atmosphere changed in a single day though, and I remember it like it was yesterday. There was a bloodbath on our street. A gang fight took place just outside our house. I can't remember for certain, but I think one kid was killed. In that moment everything was different. Suddenly it was no longer a safe environment. All of us kids took it badly, as did my parents, but for me – the youngest of the bunch – it really terrified me. For weeks and months afterwards I remember checking under the bed and in the cupboards before going to bed at night. I found it hard to sleep and was scared to go anywhere.

It was becoming a rough area, with gangs fighting and antisocial behaviour that we just weren't used to. My parents wanted us to be safe. Dad had always strived to give us a better life and worked hard to build up his businesses. He was a barber and owned a shop in Paddington, just a few doors down from where my mum worked as a seamstress. After twenty-eight years of living in England they had built a good name for themselves and had several properties under their belt, but because of these upheavals they no longer felt that they were in the right place to raise their kids.

My mum, Thea, and my dad, Savva,
back in the early eighties.

Mum and Dad had gone on holiday to Australia in 1978, just them and Debbie (being the only girl, they took Debbie with them everywhere while we boys stayed behind), and had fallen in love with it. Dad had some family already living in Sydney and initially that was where they were planning for us to settle. But while they were there some friends took them to the tropical coast and it was a case of love at first sight. It was unspoiled and less developed than Sydney, which was a big city, much more like London. They wanted to take us somewhere beautiful where there wasn't going to be any smog or violence, and the way of life, the climate, and everything else about the area appealed to them. I think they thought it would be the perfect place to escape to, that it would be great for us kids to grow up in the sunshine, on the beach, away from harm. It would be a slice of paradise.

But it wasn't an easy transition for any of us. Our parents were doing the right thing, and it was a hard decision for them to take – but for us kids it was the great unknown, a whole world away from Sudbury Court Road. My life and my friends were in England, so when my parents told me that we were moving to the other side of the world, I felt a mixture of feelings. On the one hand, it was a relief to be moving away from a place that had started to feel unsafe. But on the other hand I was gutted. Honestly, the more it sank in, the more upset I was. In hindsight it was the best decision they ever made, though I couldn't see it then. Instead, it just felt as though I was leaving everything I knew behind. I was determined to keep in touch with all my friends and I wrote to a handful of them every two weeks. I guess now it would be easy to chat to your mates even when you are the other side of the world – you've got email or MSN, but back then we were proper pen-pals and the last person I lost touch with finally was when I was fifteen.

Out of all my friends there was one person I was really upset to be leaving behind – my little Sri Lankan girlfriend, Miranda Madurasinghe. I liked her, I really did. I know it sounds silly because I was only six, but I cared for her. I can remember the butterflies like it was yesterday, so innocent and sweet but it meant everything at the time. I used to carry her satchel like a true gent! We became inseparable, both in school and out.

Me and my friend Michelle from
Benowa state high school

Once, I was naughty though. Miranda, me and her friend Cheryl got put into detention – we'd done it on purpose so that we could get thrown in the back room together. I remember kissing Miranda but then, because the lights were out, I stole the opportunity and kissed Cheryl too. They were just those magical lip kisses, no tongues, nothing like that, but they still made you all tingly. It was naughty but I was in heaven! I thought I was like the Fonz. (I seriously did – so much so, in fact, that my mum and dad had bought me a leather jacket so I could look like him! When I started a new class at school I wore it on my first day, complete with blue jeans, a white T-shirt and a comb in my back pocket. I walked into the classroom combing my hair, just like the Fonz. I thought I was a very cool dude . . . I was devastated when I outgrew it at about ten and I asked Mum and Dad to keep it for me, so that I could give it to my son one day. They did just that – for thirty years they kept it for me, how amazing is that? I brought it back from Oz earlier this year after I'd visited them for Christmas, so now it's waiting for Junior when he gets big enough. He knows about it and is already excited!)

Miranda lived close to our house and, because we spent so much time together, I couldn't imagine not being able to see her any more. To have your heart broken at six years old is pretty awful. We kept writing to each other for years. When I came back to the UK in 1992 I even looked her up. It was total luck, but I went back to Harrow, found her old house and just hoped she or her family were still living there. I knocked on the door and her mum answered. At first she didn't recognize me, but as soon as the penny dropped she was so happy to see me. Miranda wasn't there but her mum was so lovely, and she and I hatched a plan. She knew that Miranda would love to catch up with me, so we fixed a date for her to come to the studio I was working at. I wanted to wind Miranda up, so I got one of the guys at the studio to dress up and put on an Aussie accent. He combed his hair over into a side parting, put in some big false teeth and pulled his trousers up to his chest. He looked hilarious. I was hiding, so I could see everything clearly. As Miranda walked in and the pretend geeky me welcomed her you could almost see her trying to run for the hills! She was making excuses about how she didn't have long, and she'd have to leave . . . it was brilliant. I think she was recoiling in horror at what she thought I'd become. Even at six I'd had more cred than the guy who had met her. Eventually I jumped out and hugged her – she was so relieved and it turned out she didn't need to go quite so quickly after all! We chatted for ages, catching up on everything, and we became great buddies again almost immediately, as if no time had elapsed since we'd last met. I'm so glad I saw Miranda again, and although we got on brilliantly the feeling between us was pure friendship – I suppose we had both grown up. We lost touch again and I have no idea where she is now.

Emigrating to Australia was daunting but kids are resilient, and it was also kind of exciting to be moving somewhere new. The Gold Coast, Queensland, with its sunny beaches, was a world away from leafy Harrow, but what really surprised me at first was that there were *only* Aussies there. Blond-haired, blue-eyed, surfy-looking guys that the girls went crazy for. My family all had dark curly hair and dark skin, as well as London accents, so it goes without saying that we stood out in Australia with all these blond kids, big time. Locals called us wogs, which we knew was racist and bang out of order. We had never experienced any kind of prejudice before, so it was all new and horrible. Moving schools is never easy when you're a kid, but starting in a whole new country is even tougher, especially if you stand out like a sore thumb for looking different. My first day at school was not a good one. I knew straight away that it was going to be tough going. I felt lost. I wanted to go back to the UK, back to how it had been before.

Within a few days of starting school the real bullying started. It went on for a long time and became really violent. One time I was tied to a fence while a bunch of kids took it in turns to throw stones, aiming them at my head. I was terrified. At first, I never told my parents or my older brothers that I was hated because I didn't want to make things worse. Also, I knew it would upset my parents – they'd travelled here for the sake of their kids, and I wanted them to believe that I was happy and that everything was okay. When my brothers eventually found out what was going on they got involved and tried to sort the problem out – they were so protective of me – but in all honesty it only made things worse. For the first time in our lives we were experiencing racial bullying. The irony was that we'd left one country to run away from trouble and had run straight into it again in a different form.

The bullying was something I had to put up with for a long time, and even now it's hard to believe I stuck with school throughout it. Things didn't really begin to change until I was fourteen. Without my dad knowing about it, I decided to take martial arts classes and I learned very quickly how to defend myself. My heroes were Bruce Lee and, a bit later on, Jean-Claude Van Damme. They wouldn't start fights, but they'd be able to handle themselves, whatever the situation. And that was how I wanted to be. I didn't go out looking for trouble, but if trouble came to me I knew I could protect myself. (Junior has had a few lessons and has managed to get his white belt already. My brother Mike and I have taken him to classes and he loves it. When he's staying with me we practise at home. He really is quite good!) Along with my knowledge of the martial arts came a newfound confidence and eventually I was accepted at school. As time passed the area became more multicultural and my family didn't stand out in the same way.

ABOVE: ME CRABBING IN OZ AS A TEENAGER

RIGHT: JUNIOR ON A FAMILY FISHING TRIP IN 2009

Despite the bullying and the racism, the tough times brought the family closer together and I still think Australia is the most incredible place for a kid to grow up in. The weather is beautiful and we were always outdoors, playing one kind of sport or another (if the weather wasn't so good over there I don't know what they'd do! I often admire the Brits because they are so hardy – no matter what the weather they make the best of it). One of my favourite hobbies is fishing. I love it. Me, my brothers and my dad used to go to the Great Barrier Reef to fish. We'd spend hours trying to catch fish . . . obviously I always caught the biggest! My brothers Chris and Mike and I would also hang out on the pier by our house late at night to fish, with our feet dangling over the edge. As we got older we'd go out clubbing together for three or four nights a week, and then spend the other nights on the pier, hanging out together and fishing. As well as being my brothers, they really were my protectors and my friends.

Crabbing was another thing that as a child I really enjoyed – here's a picture of me at the house of our next-door neighbours looking very pleased with my catch! Look how skinny I am – that's why I used to wear those big puffa jackets in the early days! Crabs make me laugh. I was down on the beach one day with my dad when we found a crab. Dad said to me, 'See what happens when you give it a cigarette.' (Don't worry, not a lit cigarette! That would be cruel.) We found a half-smoked stub on the beach and put it down by its claw. As it walked past, the crab picked up the cigarette and as it moved sideways, as they do, it looked as though it was smoking. It was hilarious! I've always wanted to do it again and film it for *Animals Do the Funniest Things*. . . Another brilliant outdoor sport was sand-surfing: just as it sounds, you have a surf board and you surf the sand dunes, simple as that! Growing up, we'd go to Noosa Beach to do it – probably the best beach in Australia. It's beautiful and is completely natural, nothing is man-made. Sand-surfing is exhilarating and I love doing it, I get a real hit of adrenalin as I fly down the dunes. Now I do it when I go to Dubai, too, and one day the kids will love it – I know Junior will be a natural!

'NOW THAT I HAVE MY OWN CHILDREN, I LOVE TO CELEBRATE A TRADITIONAL CHRISTMAS, WHICH IS VERY DIFFERENT. FOR ME, IT'S ALL ABOUT THE KIDS AND I LOVE IT.'

Christmas Day in Australia was always a beautiful day, it was always sunny and the family would go to the beach. Where we lived on the tropical coast it was so hot, no one was going to dress up in a Santa outfit – unless this Santa had his belly out and a beer in his hand! We'd have a cold turkey lunch, cold drinks and beers for the adults, so we did celebrate it, but in our own way. Christmas time for us wasn't so much about the whole Santa Claus thing, it was about family being together and having fun. We were all brought up Jehovah's Witnesses, although Mum and Dad hadn't always been Witnesses. They used to be Greek Orthodox but switched when they had children, so we grew up in the faith, alongside my grandfather, who took it very seriously, doing three-mile walks every day, witnessing door-to-door until he was ninety-three years old! Traditionally, Witnesses don't celebrate Christmases and birthdays, but we would do things a little differently, and on birthdays we'd always get presents. On our Christmas days we'd play football together and go surfing – it was a really good laugh and one day of the year that we were all together without fail. I have really happy memories of those days. Now that I have my own children, I love to celebrate a traditional Christmas, which is very different. For me, it's all about the kids and I love it. In England the weather lends itself to the whole magical celebration and I do it all for Harvey, Junior and Princess.

Maybe more than anything else, the best thing that sticks out in my memories from my childhood in Australia is music. It's where my career first kicked off, and it's where I really began to fall in love with singing. But it's not like music was a new thing to me before we moved there. The truth is, music has been a part of my life right from the very start . . .

LIVING
THE DREAM

MY VERY EARLIEST MEMORY IS ONE LINKED TO MUSIC. IT WAS THE DAY ELVIS PRESLEY DIED. I WAS JUST FOUR YEARS OLD, WATCHING TV WITH MY FAMILY IN THE LIVING ROOM. A news flash came on and I can remember seeing the images of men and women crying, then turning around to see my dad in tears too. My father has always been a very strong, reserved man, so it was upsetting to see him like this and I wanted to stop it. Despite my dad telling me to get out of the way as I was spoiling his view, I went up to the TV and started hitting it, yelling, 'Why? Why? Why?' As I grew up I came to understand why the news had upset my dad – and millions around the world – so much. My dad loved Elvis – loved him, loved his music – but it was also that someone so young could die. When Michael Jackson died, it was a very similar thing for me, and for my son Junior, but I'll come back to that.

Music runs in the family. My grandfather Andrea was the Greek Orthodox equivalent of a gospel singer, what's called in my family's culture a 'psalmist'. People would tell him that he had the voice of an angel. A voice that was so sweet and expressive that people would beg him to sing. He was very well respected in the community and high up in the Church. He would travel from village to village and church to church, just so that people could hear his voice. My parents used to tell me that I had inherited my grandfather's voice, and its high register, but if truth be told there was a gene somewhere that we all shared. When my dad sings it's an experience to treasure, but he never liked to perform like I do, or I guess like my grandfather did. My brothers all had a passion for music, and it wasn't me but my brother Chris who was the real stand-out talented one of the bunch. He always had an incredible knack for learning instruments, and I've always looked up to him because of it.

So my brothers and I all loved music, but we had our own favourite stuff. Chris was into Santana, Dire Straits and the Stylistics, Andrew was into heavy soul, like Luther Vandross, and as for me? Well, there was only one guy that I was really obsessed with: Michael Jackson. My very first album, which I bought when I was six, was *Off the Wall*. I remember listening to it for hours, day in, day out. Songs like 'Rock with You' and 'She's Out of My Life' made a lasting impression on me that remains to this day. There was a magic about Michael Jackson – about the way he moved and sang – that I fell in love with, and from those days on he's been one of my life's biggest heroes. That love for Michael Jackson was part of a general love of Motown music. Whereas the other kids at school were getting into rock and electro-pop (this was the 1980s, remember!) I was content with the happy, soulful tunes of Smokey Robinson and Stevie Wonder.

In fact it was Stevie Wonder who was responsible for me getting that first taste of being on stage performing. Well, one of his songs, to be more precise. When I was thirteen our school was invited to take part in a talent competition. The school had a band already, complete with a singer, so when I pleaded with the music teacher to let me join in she came back saying that they already had a singer so didn't need me. I was gutted. And without wishing harm on anyone I was pretty over the moon when just before the competition was due to take place the poor singer fell sick! Tough for him, but it meant I could step in as the replacement. The competition took us to the state level, and the chance to perform Stevie's 'I Just Called to Say I Love You' in front of a thousand people. It was my first audience. We came second but that night I knew, no matter what, singing on stage was what I wanted to do for the rest of my life. I begged my father to buy me a little PA so that I could practise in the garage. I could go in there, shut the door, and practise away for hours. And I did – I'd get back home from school and go straight to the garage and spend six or seven hours singing away until nine or ten o'clock. I'd have to do my homework first, though! I knew what I wanted to do – I wanted to be a pop star – but I had to make it happen, no one else was going to do it for me. I needed to find a way of getting noticed, so I started to enter anything and everything locally to showcase my talents. I particularly remember one from when I was thirteen and I made it to the final of a Michael Jackson competition. I dressed up and looked pretty like him, or so I thought!

AGED THIRTEEN, IN THE FINAL OF
A MICHAEL JACKSON COMPETITION
IN AUSTRALIA

WITH MY BROTHERS,
ANDREW AND CHRIS.

When I was thirteen I also co-wrote my first song. I was cycling home from school and got this tune stuck in my head, 'I've been dreaming endlessly about this kind of love . . . Our very own paradise, blessed from above . . .' I loved it and figured I must have heard it before. When I got home I rushed upstairs, shouting out to Chris, 'Chris, come and listen – have you heard this before?' 'I don't know, I don't think so!' 'Then I think I've just written a song!' Chris was really great – I had a melody but didn't know what to do with it so he helped me by writing chords to go around it. 'Give me half an hour,' he said. I started working on the lyrics, and a little while later we had a song: 'Dream a Little'. About eight years later, when I recorded my first album, 'Dream a Little' was one of the songs we recorded – which really was a small dream come true. An even bigger dream came true when we performed the song on stage, five years after that, just me and Chris with his guitar, at Wembley . . .

Ironically, despite my dreams of singing success, I failed Music completely at school. I got the lowest grade in the year and the only thing that helped me justify to myself that that was sort-of okay was that Elvis, the King himself, also failed Music at school! I thought, if he can fail and still go on to have that success, maybe so can I. At school, music was all theory-based and that wasn't my strong point – I loved singing and performing. I excelled at Drama; I was the best in my year. I was a bit of a show-off, basically! And not just at school – when relatives came over to the house I'd get up on the table and sing and dance for them. I think that as the youngest of six children, I sought attention. Mum and Dad were very strict, particularly Dad with my older brothers, but they were a little bit more lenient with me. I think they had just lost patience by the time they got to me!

Junior is so like me, it's unbelievable. He does what I used to do: running around, always hugging people and wanting to kiss girls on the lips! Also, just like I was, he's very into Michael Jackson's music. He knows all the moves to some of his songs already and when we have guests over he is always performing for them. (Earlier this year I was talking to Junior and told him that I was going to do some Michael Jackson songs when I went on tour, and in his little voice he said, 'I don't want you to be Michael Jackson, I want you to be my daddy.' He is such a cute child. Then he asked me if he could meet Michael Jackson one day. I thought, 'How am I going to explain this?' He was asking me where Michael Jackson was, so many questions I didn't really know how best to answer and I just didn't know what to say. So I said he was in a lovely place and that one day, hopefully, we'd meet him. I think I got out of it, just. As my children grow up I keep getting these moments when they'll ask a difficult question and I wonder how the hell I'm going to answer!) Junior's favourite party trick is doing this Jackson dance and then saying, 'I love Michael Jackson. The girl was bad. The girl was dangerous!' I was exactly like that. I'm not sure if that's a good thing!

'JUNIOR IS SO LIKE ME. HE DOES WHAT I USED TO DO: RUNNING AROUND, ALWAYS HUGGING PEOPLE AND WANTING TO KISS GIRLS ON THE LIPS!'

When I was growing up all the kids at school were into rock. This was Australia in the 1980s and AC/DC was playing everywhere – it was a rock market. At the time that kind of music was strongly associated with violence. That might seem weird now, but it was all about headbanging! Long hair, violence, fighting, heavy drinking and all that. Which is fine, but there was an aggressiveness to it, which I never really took to. Nowadays I love that kind of stuff – I've hung out with Angus Young and Robert Plant and they're great guys – and I know several ageing rock stars who are more interested in gardening than anything else (it hasn't happened to me! Yet ...). I've even started introducing a bit of rock into my music and my shows.

But the 1980s obsession with rock was a problem for me, because as I started taking part in local talent competitions, singing Motown songs like 'Stand by Me' in pubs and bars, the audiences just weren't getting it. It's not that it didn't go down well but the judges would always say, 'It's not what we're looking for.' Which, let's face it, is normally what someone says when they think you're crap! It was obvious that no one was going to give out a prize for performing soul or jazz ...

T hen a couple of my friends told me about a show called *New Faces*. I didn't know it then but it was something that would change my life. It was an Australian TV show that was a bit like *Britain's Got Talent*. If you were around at the time, you might remember the British version, which launched the careers of household names like Lenny Henry, Victoria Wood and Michael Barrymore. You didn't have to be a singer, and you didn't have to sing a particular type of music. You could be a dancer, an actor – it was all about giving people an opportunity to showcase their talent. But just like *X Factor* nowadays, and *Pop Idol* before that, it was hard on kids because there was so much expectation. I owe everything to a TV talent show, so I'm not knocking it, but the rise is very big and very quick and the fall is also very big, very quick and very hard. I don't think people realize what that feels like or can prepare themselves for it before they go on these shows. I know I didn't. To have fame and then to lose it is very difficult to deal with.

But back then, *New Faces* was an opportunity for my dreams of becoming a pop star to come true. My buddies at school were constantly telling me, 'Go on it! You should do it! You'd be great at it! They won't mind that you're not singing rock songs!' But I didn't have the courage. Singing in front of a camera? On TV? In front of millions of people? You must be kidding. Funnily enough, even now, if you put me on stage in front of thousands of people I'll be fine, but put me in front of a TV camera and I'll freeze – it's a totally different thing. So I let the opportunity to audition pass. Until it was too late. When I finally found the courage to give it a go they'd taken the show off air, and weren't planning on recommissioning it. I got hold of the number for the people at the show and every Monday morning for weeks on end I'd call up, begging them, 'If the show ever comes back on would you audition me?' Given that they'd taken the show off air you'd probably think I was a bit crazy. Especially as I was making excuses to come in a couple of hours late to school every week just so I could make those phone calls. You might ask what kept me calling them up, and although I didn't know it then I guess I was practising what I now know as 'The Secret'.

When you're young there are certain things that you just know are going to happen. There's this thing called The Secret which I apply a lot of the time – you might have heard of it. It's based on the law of attraction: attracting the right things into your life. I've read the books, watched the documentaries and have a really good understanding of it. I really believe that it works. If you think positively, good things can happen. If you believe in something and visualize that 'something' enough then it will materialize. Bear with me, this does make sense! I'm sure everyone can think of something that they just knew would come true for them. Even before I had ever sung in public, a part of me believed that one day I would sell out Wembley Arena. Years later, I did it. What I'm trying to say is that The Secret works. Believe in something enough, imagine and visualize it enough and it will happen, providing you don't lose faith and start to doubt it. You must never doubt. When it does happen, you may think it is just coincidence, but who cares how it happened? Just be happy that it did happen.

So, finally the good news that I'd been hoping for came and my own faith and belief paid off – they were putting the show back on and I was going to get a chance to audition. The first auditions for *New Faces* were in Queensland. I was beside myself, despite my dad's reservations. Dad wasn't keen at all on the idea of me going into the music industry – he wanted me to have a proper job like an architect or a doctor, something more sensible than trying to be a pop star. He thought I was trying to live a pipe dream. I had already annoyed him by running up the phone bill with my continuous calls to the TV station, and he thought I was wasting his time as well as mine. It didn't stop me, though, and I finally had the audition that I had dreamed of for so many months. What happened next was unbelievable and changed my life for ever.

After getting through the auditions I had my chance to sing for the judging panel. In the waiting room I was so scared. The vibe among the contestants was majorly tense. I nearly bottled it – there were tears and all sorts. I sang Bobby Brown's 'Don't be Cruel' for the judges, with a dance routine and everything. I had had the whole thing choreographed by my brother's mate Victor so I was prepared but my confidence had left the building! Deep down, I knew I could do it but I was worried I'd mess it all up under pressure. There was an ad break before I got the judges' verdict and those were the longest three minutes of my life.

Eventually they were ready. As they started to give their feedback it took a couple of seconds to register what they were saying. They were giving positive comments! Even better, these were followed finally by one judge, Ian 'Molly' Meldrum, offering me a contract live on air. I couldn't believe it. Not only had I been given the thumbs up, I had been given a record contract too!

The next day I kept thinking, I bet they're regretting it, I bet they wish they hadn't done that. My excitement turned to worry. I'm sure everyone at the label was going mad at Molly, telling him that he couldn't just sign someone without knowing more about them, but he stood by me. He said he saw something in me. Molly ended up becoming my manager and he catapulted me into the limelight. He was the man in Australia, the Simon Cowell of the day. If he approved of you, then you were going to make it big.

After the show, I didn't hear anything for six months from Molly or his team and I began getting worried. I thought they had forgotten me and I just couldn't understand why they hadn't been in touch. I was new to the business and I didn't understand then how long it takes record companies to sort these things out.

Meanwhile, I decided to put on a charity concert at school. Everyone was excited because 'one of their own' had been in the national newspapers and on national TV, so there was a real buzz about it when they heard I'd be performing at the school. I organized a half-hour lunchtime concert for charity – my first solo performance – charging 50 cents per person. We filled out the hall completely. On the back of it, I decided to do another concert at the Gold Coast Arts Theatre, which seated a thousand people. Would a thousand people come and see me, and actually buy tickets? I had no idea, and I was worried that they wouldn't. This would be a real test. But sure enough, it sold out too. Me and my brother Chris and my friend Loreen Land put the show together. We called it 'ANDRE PRODUCTIONS PRESENTS PETER ANDRE LIVE IN CONCERT FOR ONE NIGHT ONLY!' As you can tell, we took it pretty seriously! And one thing about the show really was serious – a guy from the record company came up to watch it. I hadn't signed the deal yet, so to have a guy there to see what I'd achieved was important, as it would show that my performance on TV hadn't just been fluke. 'You know what,' he said, 'whether we sign you up or not isn't the point . . . You've got something, and it works.' I'd been so worried about whether *New Faces* was a flash in a pan. I wanted to prove that I deserved that contract – that I had the commitment to make it work – and 'ANDRE PRODUCTIONS' had done just that.

F inally the call from the record company came, and boy was I happy. But nothing was going to happen just yet. I didn't know at the time but my dad had spoken to the record company and said to them, 'Look, you can do what you want with his singing but only after he's finished school.' That was a while away. So despite be ing impatient to get on with my new pop career I had school to finish off. Looking back now I feel so grateful to my dad. Education isn't just important, it's king. And my dad knew it. He was protecting me, in the same way that I hope I can protect my kids in the future. To let them follow their dreams, but make sure that they're safe to do so. It was the same with money. I never cared about money and to tell the truth, it's never been a priority – for me, the importance of money nowadays is all about how I can help prepare for my kids' future. For me the singing was about the music and the performing. So when I finally signed that contract I didn't have a clue what I was doing or what I should do with the money. My dad kept it. For me. He looked after it, investing it, so that it would be there to support me if anything bad happened and the dream of success fell flat.

It felt like an age before I released any music. I found it frustrating, two years seemed like for ever. But things were definitely happening. I became more popular and girls started to pay me attention (despite my mullet!) and I liked it. The martial arts and working out that I'd been doing had paid off big time and I felt good about the way I looked. I would hang out with my mates in bars and clubs. We were pretty wild – we enjoyed the drinking and the girls. And as much as I was having fun, I did feel guilty about what I was getting up to. Religion has always played a part in my life, but as I grew up I found it hard to reconcile the life I was beginning to lead with my parents' beliefs. I came to understand that I wasn't going to follow in my grandfather's footsteps, and I gradually started to skip our weekly Witness meetings every Sunday. I didn't want to be a hypocrite. Then, when I was seventeen, I had my first proper sexual relationship and I stopped practising altogether. Because of my physical intimacy with this girl I was seeing I felt as though I had betrayed my beliefs. We didn't have a massive family row about it – I had made my mind up and that was that. I still respect Mum and Dad's beliefs: they have instilled good values in all of us, and for me family will always come first.

ME IN SYDNEY APRIL 1993, AGED TWENTY

'FINALLY THE RECORD COMPANY TOLD ME THEY WERE SENDING ME TO ENGLAND TO RECORD MY FIRST SONG. I COULDN'T STOP JUMPING UP AND DOWN, I WAS SO EXCITED.'

Finally the record company told me they were sending me to England to record my first song. I couldn't stop jumping up and down, I was so excited. They flew me over and put me up in a hotel where Kylie Minogue was staying. She was in the process of making it big in the UK, and although the songs I was working on were only about to be released in Oz it gave me a taste of what the future could hold. The first song we worked on was 'Drive Me Crazy', which was the second song I'd ever written. The video we filmed for it was a bit like a male version of *Flashdance*, with me dancing away in an empty warehouse. If you look at the video now you might not believe me, but the way I was dressed up was pretty cool for the time – the vest-top, the 'rustic' look . . . It got to number seventy-two in the charts, which wasn't particularly pleasing.

My next single changed everything though. 'Gimme Little Sign' was the turning point for my career. It was a big success, just like 'Mysterious Girl' was going to be in the UK. It was the sixth biggest selling single of the decade in Australia. To be honest, it wasn't the music that made the difference, it was the video. My look had changed completely. I'd made a conscious decision to use my inspirations – Michael Jackson and Jean-Claude Van Damme – and mix them together to make something new. Why not combine image, dance, music and singing to create something new? I knew my physique attracted the girls, so why not show it off while I was performing? The only guy that I'd seen who was doing this was Mark Wahlberg, or Marky Mark as he was known back then, and people were going crazy for his music as well as his ripped, sexy look. But he was a rapper, and I thought, 'No one's doing that in pop music.' The music company didn't want me to do it, but I just said, 'Guys, why can't it work? It's worked for him.' And I was right. The video is what sold the song. And it wasn't the first time that it would do so. I knew that my look, and having my abs on display, was as important as the catchiness of the song. It's no wonder that over the next few years I'd become more and more obsessed with maintaining this image – right from the very start of my career I got used to associating it with keeping the fans happy.

Things were going from strength to strength, and before long I released my first album. I was really proud of it, it was yet another dream come true for me. The success of 'Gimme Little Sign' had also led to something incredible happening. I was given the chance to join Bobby Brown's Australian tour. Back then, he was the coolest guy you could imagine – like 50 Cent or Jay-Z nowadays. Just to meet him was a dream come true. For the kid that had been the odd one out at school it finally felt like I'd been accepted. I'd joined the cool gang. I also went on tour with Madonna, which was awesome. The best moment was the Melbourne gig, in front of a packed crowd of eighty thousand people. It was a clear, beautiful night. I was working with a band called CDB, made up of a group of brilliant vocalists. We performed 'In the Still of the Night' a cappella and you could hear a pin drop. I'll never forget that feeling of silence erupting into applause. For me, that was one of the biggest highlights of my life.

It wasn't all cheers though. The low point on that tour came when I was leaving one of the venues. People started hurling abuse at the car. It was something that would happen again – and sometimes I'd leave a venue not knowing whether I'd be cheered or insulted, abused or praised. There was no other young kid having this kind of success in Australia at that time, and it was obvious that there were as many people out there who took against me as there were fans. Maybe some of the guys were jealous of the attention I was getting from women. Perhaps it was that, but I think it was also simply that a lot of people didn't like me. Sometimes you can't be everyone's cup of tea, and although it was really hard to take at the time I can accept that now.

It was going to get a whole lot worse before it got better, and I had one horrendous experience in Sydney when a gang surrounded me and pulled out knives, threatening me. It made me not want to walk the streets again. I also had knives pulled on me in clubs, which began to make me associate them with violence. I used to love going to clubs – it had been my escape, and then all of a sudden I couldn't escape because I thought I was in more danger there. It was a horrific time, and when I had a breakdown years later I think a lot of it was because of those times.

I felt like I had to get out of Australia. I thought to myself, 'Just leave . . . Go somewhere where they don't know you, and start again.' It was crazy in a way, for if I'd stayed there I could have done even better, but I wanted to leave when I was on top because I was scared of it being taken away. I'd always dreamed of performing at Wembley Arena and I wanted to have a crack at gaining a fanbase in the UK. Thankfully, the record company agreed to send me to the UK to record and produce my second album.

Coming to England after the massive success in Australia was quite weird. I went from not being able to walk down the street without minders to nobody really knowing me or recognizing me. In a way it was quite nice to have that anonymity back, but I was young and ambitious and I wanted to make it big over here too – and nothing was going to stop me! Even having a steady girlfriend in Australia called Kathy didn't stop me from wanting to be in England pursuing my dream.

I recorded a few tracks for the new album that would be released in Australia – after all, I was here to do that – but it wasn't long before I started to push for a bit more. I wanted to try to get a fanbase for myself here in the UK. The record label I was on, Melodian/Mushroom Records, was very small. I was literally begging them to release my music in the UK but they kept telling me it wasn't going to work. I was unstoppable, though, and determined to be listened to, so I asked them if they'd let me do some Under-18 appearances. Brilliantly, they agreed. They said they'd only pay me £10 a night, and I'd have to pay for my own petrol, but I didn't care, it was my chance. So they gave me a little Peugeot and I went and did some gigs. There I was in Oz with drivers, bodyguards, the whole entourage, and I'd come to England and had to start all over again! I didn't care, though, I was willing to do anything – I had the belief and I needed to give myself the opportunity to prove it to those around me. I'd turn up at a gig and no one would know me, but by the end of each evening I would cause hysteria in the audience, and before we knew it letters were flying in to Mushroom Records, asking them to release my material. They got thousands and thousands of letters, and it didn't take too long for them to sit up and take notice, and realize this could be big. You could almost see them thinking, 'We'd better release something!'

'Turn It Up' was my first British release and it hobbled into the charts at number sixty-four. But, like I say, my determination knew no bounds. I wanted to keep releasing material until I became a household name. I knew it was possible; after all, the gigs were more popular than ever and there was mayhem wherever we went. I felt that I was achieving some of my dreams, but I was working really hard to do that, and only getting five or six hours' sleep a night. I think my life's busy now, but back then it was really full on!

Something had to change, and little did I know it but I was just about to meet someone very special . . .

COMING HOME

I T WAS AT ONE OF THE GIGS ON THE ISLE OF WIGHT THAT I MET CLAIRE POWELL. CLAIRE AND HER THEN BUSINESS PARTNER, SUE HARRIS, OWNED A MANAGEMENT COMPANY CALLED BLITZ MANAGEMENT. THEY HAD A REPUTATION FOR PUTTING ON THESE AMAZING ROADSHOWS AND DISCOVERING NEW TALENT, SO HELEN AT MUSHROOM RECORDS THOUGHT CLAIRE WOULD BE THE BEST PERSON TO GET MY MUSIC HEARD. Claire agreed to put me onstage at the Isle of Wight and it couldn't have gone better. The crowds were going wild and straight after the performance, Claire came backstage to find me. Everyone had spoken about her as this lovely, tough but caring mum figure, and I could understand what they meant straight away. Claire said she wanted to manage me – she said she could see that I had a future in the UK and she wanted to make me a success. But I had to end it with my management in Australia first. Our contract was up for renewal so technically I was unmanaged at the time, but I was nervous because I knew that wasn't going to be an easy conversation. I had been stung once and wanted to be sure that this was the right thing for me to do. I decided to get my dad involved – I wanted him to oversee the contracts and the details so I faxed everything over to him in Australia. Dad liked the sound of Claire; he said that she would be good for me and make me a success and he was right. I needed time to think about it, to decide what was right for me and my career, but my dad was on side and really it was his approval that I was after. Claire continued to call, and she wrote this big proposal including all the plans she had for me. After much discussion we agreed that she would manage me. It was all very businesslike! She put so much effort in, I couldn't have asked for more. The time had come for me to make the call to Molly, as I knew I needed to tell him, which was actually a lot easier than I imagined. I was now living in England full-time, my career was flying and I needed to be here permanently. Yet another move for me, but one that I really wanted to make.

M y new manager was on it straight away. Claire realized how important it was to develop my fanbase and she came up with the idea that I could do school tours. I'd be booked for an assembly, for a lunch break or after school had finished, and would perform and then do a question-and-answer session about how I'd got into the music industry and how I wanted to stay away from drugs. It was really well received. We would hand out cards for people to sign up to my fan club and eventually we produced a small fanzine. I had about eighty thousand fans within weeks.

I started touring on the *Mizz* magazine roadshow, which was being headlined by Sean Maguire, who at the time was pretty massive. Before I went on we dropped a huge forty-foot poster of me on to the stage – the crowd went crazy. I was due onstage as the fourth act, but the crowds were going so mad that they had to move my slot, so I came on just before Sean. I can remember the screams as I went onstage as though it were yesterday. Soon afterwards I had the massive privilege of going on tour with the boy band East 17. They had huge street cred at the time (they were a bit like the equivalent of N-Dubz: I sometimes think Dappy looks a little like Brian Harvey, especially with the choice in hats!). I got on really well with the boys and we've stayed friends ever since.

The tours had built a fanbase, but just around the corner was something that would put me on the map in a major way.

I WAS THE SUPPORT ACT ON THE EAST 17
TOUR SHORTLY AFTER I ARRIVED IN THE
UK. BRIAN HARVEY WAS A REALLY GOOD
GUY WHO HELPED ME AT THE BEGINNING
OF MY CAREER IN THE UK

WE FILMED THE VIDEO FOR 'MYSTERIOUS GIRL' IN PHUKET, THAILAND

My memories of working on 'Mysterious Girl' are nothing but full of bliss, and shooting the film was one of the best times of my life. People probably think of the video and think of me, the sunshine and of the girl in the waterfall. Well, there's a story there. Behind the scenes there really was a proper tropical romance going on. The girl in the video, whose name is Champagne, was someone I'd met briefly before, but I had no idea when I flew out to Thailand that she'd be appearing in the film. We clicked and pretty much started dating right there and then, before the filming even began. Everything about the week we spent there was incredible – the weather, the people, and of course Champagne. One night, as we were sailing back from the island where we'd been filming to Phuket, underneath a starlit sky, we ran out of petrol. We were stranded in the ocean. It was scary, but the romance of the situation soon replaced any fear we had about making it back to dry land. I guess I'd describe it as being a bit like the film Titanic, but with much warmer water (and thankfully, we survived!).

When we got back to England and released the song we had trouble getting the radios to pick it up, and at first it charted at just fifty-three. We thought, 'Okay, that's not so bad,' but we all felt that something was around the corner. Sure enough, we were soon getting phone calls telling us that The Box, the music video channel, had started playing it and that it was shooting up the charts. Before we knew it, it was at the top spot and stayed there for twelve weeks. We were amazed – The Box normally only played American artists. Then, when I was on my next tour, with Boyzone, we discovered that the single had gone in at number three in the singles chart. For the second time in my career, a video – and, let's face it, the abs! – had really helped boost my success. Two other singles released afterwards, 'Flava' and 'I Feel You', went to the number-one spot. I couldn't believe it. I'd cracked the UK.

I wanted it to be the best show possible so I even travelled to Vegas to get some ideas. I wanted it to be something that everyone would remember. In the event, it turned out to be truly out of this world. Before I came on stage the whole arena was blanketed in darkness. Then, to simulate a spaceship taking off, a countdown began. The hysteria in the auditorium worked up to a fever pitch and when I finally came on stage and slowly removed my black sunglasses from my face it felt like the noise was going to blow the roof of the auditorium straight off! The show really was stupendous, but my memory of it is not without regrets. When I arrived at the venue I remember looking up and thinking, 'Oh my god, it's really happening.' And I should have revelled in the moment. But I felt under so much pressure at the time that I couldn't really enjoy it. As time passes, I'm able to appreciate the memories more and more. The comedown after Wembley was tough. I don't know if you've ever achieved your ultimate goal, but for me it was Wembley, and I didn't have a plan for what I should do afterwards. It may sound strange, but if you'd asked me 'So what do you want to do next?' I wouldn't have had an answer. I simply didn't know. While professionally I was at my highest, personally things were gradually starting to unravel at the seams.

'I WANTED IT TO BE SOMETHING THAT EVERYONE WOULD REMEMBER. IN THE EVENT, IT TURNED OUT TO BE TRULY OUT OF THIS WORLD'

There were high points still to come though. At the World Music Awards in Monaco, I even got to meet the woman of my dreams – Halle Berry. I have always been attracted to black girls, ever since my very first girlfriend, Miranda, and Halle Berry is just gorgeous. We had our picture taken together but I was so nervous, I was shaking. Afterwards I asked Claire to get hold of that picture for me. It's a wonderful memory; she is such a beautiful woman. There were so many big names there – when I went onstage and looked down I could see in the front row Lionel Richie, Céline Dion, Halle Berry and the Prince of Monaco. I have never felt so intimidated. The after-party was incredible; it was one of the best parties I've ever been to, with celebrities including Boyzone, All Saints and Bros, as well as big actors and singers from the States. It was held on a huge yacht that had four jet skis, a casino and a black helicopter. Caviar was served on ice sculptures – it was jaw-droppingly amazing and I felt so privileged to be there. After that trip I really fell in love with Monaco and I've been back many times since.

With the touring and my growing workload, my gruelling transatlantic schedule was soon to cause me trouble. I was getting sucked into the lurid world of the celebrity lifestyle. I was becoming obsessed with the way I looked, because the better I appeared, the better the sales and the more female attention I received. And it was becoming a problem. When I'd first started working out as a kid I was doing it for myself – to bulk out, to put the bullies off taking me on, to appeal to the girls, to go from being the odd one out to being the one they wanted to be with. And I'd done it all for me. But now I was doing it just to maintain what I thought people wanted to see. I was also developing an obsession with America that was growing, constantly nagging at the back of my mind. It felt like it was the next uncharted territory to tackle. Meanwhile, I felt the record company were losing interest in me and weren't taking my ideas and thoughts into consideration. They were interested in the commercial aspect, granted, but I wanted to be able to have a bit of a say in my next move and what I was doing. In many ways it was crazy for me to feel like this because I was having so much success, but I was young and ambitious and I thought, 'If I can be this successful in Australia, and in the UK and Europe, surely I can do it in the States?' I'd already done twelve sell-out tour dates in Germany, and had my own tour in Switzerland, Australasia, Dubai, Bahrain, France, Spain and Holland, so I thought I would definitely have success elsewhere. Arrogance, maybe, was getting in the way of the right thing to do. I was becoming increasingly unhappy even though I had the success I'd always wanted. I wanted to try to prove myself to a different market. But I was exhausted from the sell-out tour and felt I needed a break. However, it seemed like a break was the last thing I was going to get.

At the Music Awards in Monaco

ABOVE: WITH MY BROTHER, MIKE ON VENICE BEACH, LA, WHILST SHOOTING THE VIDEO FOR 'ALL ABOUT US' FROM THE ALBUM *TIME*

My next album – my third – was called *Time*. Ironically, looking back, it was the one thing I didn't have! I barely had time to catch my breath between the second and third albums, and we were soon back in the recording studio laying down tracks and out filming. One of the video shoots was for a track we released as a single, called 'Lonely', and it saw us shooting across to Arizona. The location was in the middle of the desert and we were told we had to be really careful to stick to the road and not go past the fences because the Native Americans owned the land so it's not under US law enforcement. But I really wanted to cross the line to film, it was so beautiful – I wanted to get the mountains in shot, it was the perfect backdrop. The driver was adamant that he wouldn't go past the fences and he started to tell us the story of someone else who had done it, how the Native Americans had come and taken all their film away and kept them overnight. But I did it anyway! We thought no one would come and we would be quick. We took the coach over the line and they started filming me standing on the roof, wearing this massive Donna Karan coat. I was so nervous, I thought the Indians were gonna come and get me. I was on edge anyway, and then this Native American war-cry noise suddenly sounded. I was terrified. I practically vaulted off the lorry I was so scared; I have never moved so quickly. It was my mate, Dean Stratten winding us all up! Afterwards it really was very funny but at the time I didn't think so, I can tell you. But I still smile remembering that story.

It had been baking hot all day – a local told me it hadn't rained at this time of year for fifty years. But within an hour the sky had turned black with dark storm clouds. As we drove towards the airport the heavens opened and the worst storm I have ever seen started. Lightning was hitting telegraph poles and sending thunderbolts right across the front of our truck. I was thinking quietly to myself, 'With all the things that have happened over the past few days, do I really want to be getting on this plane?' In fact, I was so worried that we wouldn't make it back that I phoned my parents just in case something happened. We got on the plane, and as it took off we all linked hands, praying that we would get there in one piece. The ride was seriously bumpy, which was extremely frightening. It had been a weird couple of days. I had successfully written a new album and we were on our way back to the UK, but somehow I felt that there was a bigger storm on the horizon. This time it wasn't one that I could see or feel, but I knew it was there. And it wasn't going to be something we could just fly through and escape from. I somehow knew, I guess it was a gut feeling, that the road ahead wasn't going to lead to a bed of roses.

Although my career was reaching an all-time high, I was beginning to believe the hype and my feet weren't as firmly attached to the ground as they should have been. I felt like I was an icon and I started living like one. The worst thing you can do is to believe the hype surrounding you. To quote an old saying, 'It'll all end in tears' – and sure enough, it did. Already the signs were showing that mentally I wasn't in the best shape. I started to get panic attacks and my need to run away to what I thought was a safer place became top of my priority list. Crazy really, given the effort I had put in to make it big here, and then I wanted to go somewhere else. Work that one out, because I can't! The fame bug eats you alive: it really is here one day and gone the next. This time round I'm a lot calmer and although it's bigger now than ever I know I can't do everything. I have kids and they come first.

So running away was what I did . . .

I part-owned a resort with my mum and dad called Bribie Island, an island just off the coast of Australia, by Brisbane. My parents had made some good business decisions, and they were building up quite a property portfolio by this stage. They worked incredibly hard for it and this was just another string to their bow. You could think that I was born with a silver spoon in my mouth, but I wasn't. We were never spoiled but taught the value of money. When things started to go wrong for me I fled to Bribie Island for some normality. I was waiting tables, cleaning and mucking in at the resort alongside all my family. Three days into my stay, when I thought I was finding happiness again, I fell apart.

During a family meal with my parents, enjoying the sort of moment that should have been peaceful and happy, I started shaking. Out of nowhere my mind became flooded with images of me hurting myself. It was terrifying. I ran to my room crying and shaking. I had lost it. Mum called my brothers home and when they arrived they knew immediately that I needed urgent help. I was rushed to hospital and I can remember thinking, 'How the hell has this happened?' It felt like I'd lost everything. The doctors let me go home that night and told me to relax, but that was just the beginning of a terrifying time for me. For two years I suffered up to twenty panic attacks a day. My only escape was when I was sleeping so I would often spend up to eighteen hours a day asleep. I tried to help myself and made appointments with doctors and people I thought could help, yet none of them seemed to get it. The one thing that did make sense was being told that anxiety comes at times of peace and calm. You might think that returning home, to the open arms of my parents and family, would have put me into a happier state. And it did, but it was the first time I'd had any breathing space or time to think for such a long while. The trauma of the threats I'd received in Australia was something I'd bottled away. Now, having taken a step back from it all, the lid was coming off. I was alone, very alone, and so I did the only thing I seemed to know how to do: keep on the move.

This time I went to New York. My brothers Chris and Mike came with me, and I called on a few people there that I knew and started looking for work again, back in the industry that had got me into this state in the first place. I was determined to crack America – there was no stopping me. Even Claire, who was usually so supportive and would always make me see sense, couldn't change my mind. I knew that if I went to the US against her advice our partnership would be finished. Her true words ring in my ears even now. She said to me that she knew she had to set me free, that I had to fly my wings. I thought the grass was greener and she knew that it wasn't, but because I wouldn't listen she had to let me go, let me experience it and understand that ultimately it was the wrong thing to do. She was right. But at the time I wanted to live the American Dream – something lots of British artists try to do and fail miserably. Why do we all chase something else? Why can't we be happy with our lot? But the first time round on the fame game I was greedy and hungry for more. Looking back, things were going so well for me in the UK and yet I couldn't wait to get to America and break it. At that stage in my life I chose to do the exact opposite of what I was advised, something I regret now. My contract with Blitz was coming to an end so, quite stupidly, I decided that I would try to go it alone, based on a load of false promises from other managers. I felt awful when I told Claire that she wouldn't be managing me any more: she had done so much for me over the years, I knew this hurt her and I felt terrible, but I thought it was what I had to do. Ideally I wanted her to come with me and join up with an American manager but she had a big PR company too so couldn't give it all up, which I understood. So we went our separate ways.

Claire has given a lot up for me over the years – not many managers would leave their home to go on tour with you and make sure you are looked after every step of the way. When she was younger and didn't have a family it was easier for her to do that. We've always got on really well and being on tour together was a laugh. Claire is like a sister to me. My family and Claire's family are very close, like one big happy family, and her son is great friends with Junior and Tiaamii. Even now, Claire, Neville – her boyfriend and business partner – and everyone at the company, Can Associates, are hands-on and make sure that everything goes smoothly. Since the split with Katie, both Claire and Nicola Partridge have been pillars of strength. Believe me, they have come under some heavy fire and criticism themselves, which hasn't been fair at all. Over the years Claire and I have become great friends and I totally trust her but our friendship has never got in the way of her managing me. She is an absolute professional and will never shy away from telling me things that are hard to hear. She's honest and fair, and those qualities, I have learned, are very good ones to have in your manager. It's very easy to say what your client wants to hear, it's not so easy telling them the truth.

When I was with Katie, it's true that my relationship with my management could get a bit strained. You see, it was nearly always Katie's way and what she wanted, and that made things difficult at times. Towards the end of our relationship, Claire didn't feel comfortable coming over to our house to socialize. In fact, she only came to our Woldingham home once for dinner. I think she felt a bit awkward. Now, we go out as families, we do a lot more things together. We take the kids out and see each other for Sunday dinners – it's more relaxed for everyone. I know that when I started to make it big in England the first time round, there was a part of me that started to get a bit arrogant, but I have learned from that. I would never be like that now, no way. I think I'm so lucky to have what I've got so why would I want to risk it all? My fans are incredibly important – without fans all of us in the public eye would be nothing. I can only thank the public for the support they have given me over the years, but particularly of late. I still wake up and pinch myself over their loyalty.

At this point, though, my main loyalty was to my ambition . . .

With Nicola Partridge, Katie and Claire
Powell — we were on our way to Ascot
in June 2008

RUNNING AWAY, AGAIN

TO MAKE IT IN AMERICA I SIGNED WITH BIG MANAGERS WHO PROMISED THE WORLD. THEY SET UP MEETINGS WITH COCA-COLA, PEPSI, MCDONALDS, THE LOT, AND THEY WERE ALL WILLING TO GET ON BOARD AND BECOME PART OF MY SUCCESS STORY STATESIDE. BUT, OF COURSE, WHEN IT CAME TO THE CRUNCH NO ONE DID ANYTHING. False promises were a sign of things to come and when Claire and I went our separate ways I was suddenly very vulnerable. I met with two agents, Lou Pearlman and Johnny Wright. Johnny is an incredible manager and at the time was managing the Backstreet Boys and 'N Sync. The Backstreet Boys were a new boy band who were becoming very popular and successful. When I tell you this story you're probably not going to believe me, but it's the God's honest truth. I met with Johnny and he said he was looking for a young guy to break America. He wanted someone who could sing and dance and he said he'd seen what I could do. He said he needed to work with me to polish me, change my style a bit, and his final words were, 'I'll make you massive.' I was so excited, I thought, 'This is it – I am going to make it big time' – but my dreams were very quickly dashed when Johnny failed to turn up for our next meeting. When I was able to get hold of him he said he had reconsidered the situation, because he didn't want to step on my management's toes. The management that I was no longer with. I was totally gutted. Johnny also had his eye on someone else. That was Justin Timberlake, who of course is now a megastar. Johnny knew what he wanted, had a vision, and then plucked JT out of 'N Sync and made him into a superstar. I couldn't help thinking, 'What if?', because word for word what he said he was going to do, he did . . . just not with me. Fate, I guess.

All was not lost, though, because Lou Pearlman also wanted to sign me. Again, just like Johnny, he said he wanted to make me into a big star and I fell for that hook, line and sinker. By this point I had become quite good friends with the Backstreet Boys, who were warning me off Lou. They told me they had just opened their own label and that they would sign me. My first gig would be to tour with them as their support group, which would have given me massive exposure. Stupidly, I turned them down – I needed guidance and I hadn't got management to advise me at the time. I believed in Lou and was loyal to him, but nothing ever materialized and I felt hugely let down. He seemed like such a nice guy, but several years on he was sent to prison for fraud, so I'm not exactly a great judge of character!

It is one of my biggest regrets in life that I didn't tour with the Backstreet Boys and sign to their label. If I had, perhaps I could have cracked America. Instead it was the most depressing time of my life and a tough lesson to learn the hard way. For this reason, this time round I have promised myself that I will be happy with what I have. I think I have finally learned that hard lesson. Claire recently asked me about going into Europe and testing the market there, but to be honest it makes me nervous. Look how busy I am: is this something I really need to do? Five weeks in Germany trying to promote, six weeks somewhere else . . . do I really need to do it? I've got my kids and I wouldn't want to be away from them for such a long period of time. My priorities have changed and I'm content.

Thinking back to those days, there was a lot of wild stuff going on and a lot of bands coming up through the ranks. One of them was The Spice Girls. While 'Flava' was riding high in the charts, they were getting ready to release 'Wannabe', a song that would catapult them to the top. Around that time I started seeing Mel B, or Scary Spice as she was known back then. Let me just say, Mel is awesome and we are good friends now. But our relationship was volatile, to say the least – it was very different to anything I'd had before with a woman. She was full on. In my last book I was fairly frank and open about what went on and I feel bad about having done that now. Mel and I have made up since then. It's in the past and we are good mates now, that's all that matters.

At the same time that I stopped seeing Mel B, my album *Time* didn't do nearly as well as I'd hoped it would in the UK – charting at a disappointing number twenty-seven. (I did have two Top Five singles from that album, but I'd wanted to be more credible so in the videos I wasn't taking my top off . . . and perhaps that had a negative effect on the overall album sales.) I hid myself away for three days when that happened, obsessing about anything and everything. I started to focus again on my body, exercising at every available opportunity – once I even did push-ups and sit-ups on a plane while everyone else was sleeping, that's how crazy it got for me.

I was still hooked on the idea of America, big time – I had the bug. I was dressing in baggy clothes which were very trendy over there at the time and I was influenced by everything USA. I really thought that with persistence I could crack it. As it was becoming increasingly clear, it was all a big mistake. I was there for two years recording music, but despite the promises from those around me nothing happened. To this day I still have a feeling of 'unfinished business' towards America. I never had a chance even to test the waters, as nothing was ever released . . . The whole time I was away from Claire's management I didn't release anything, not even one track. The dream had gone belly up and living in hotels was once again getting to me. I was really low; it felt like I was heading on a downward spiral towards breakdown. I didn't want to be in America and I didn't want to be in England, so I headed back to Australia, the place I had run from originally.

ON HOLIDAY IN CYPRUS, 2009 WITH TIAAMII, JUNIOR, HARVEY, MY MUM AND MY BROTHER MIKE.

I wanted to be with my family again, away from the industry that had all but broken me. I needed time to sort myself out and heal properly. I had been working the fame machine from such a young age, and it had finally got to me. I'm not blaming anyone because it was what I wanted – to sing, perform, write music – but the industry is tough and to have such success and then lose it is bloody hard. When you first dream of making it big you don't necessarily think of the money, you think more about the fame, about being onstage and doing what you love for a living. So when you first achieve your dream you are so grateful, so excited. But that feeling soon goes and I think nearly everyone who's experienced it, if they're being honest, goes through a period of being arrogant, taking for granted what they've got and thinking that it will never end. But end it sure does. And when it does, it's hard. If I were to give advice to someone starting now, I'd tell them to keep good friends and family around them to ensure they stay grounded. I'd say, don't get caught up in it all. This industry sounds so glamorous but once you're in it there's a dark side that you can very easily get caught up in. I am pretty levelled generally, particularly these days, but back in the day I was definitely a victim of success. It was different back then, you had to travel to a different country daily to keep it all going.

> 'IF I WERE TO GIVE ADVICE TO SOME-ONE STARTING NOW, I'D TELL THEM TO KEEP GOOD FRIENDS AND FAMILY AROUND THEM TO ENSURE THEY STAY GROUNDED. I'D SAY, DON'T GET CAUGHT UP IN IT ALL.'

Claire didn't know how bad my situation was and how bad things had got, but as we started to speak a bit more regularly, and gradually as I sorted myself out, I thought about making a proper return to the music business. I was nervous because fundamentally I was frightened of the industry; I felt my life had become easier being away from the limelight, but on the flip side I was beginning to miss it. I hadn't released anything for five years so a comeback was daunting. I'd had time out, time that had been forced upon me because of my health, but in a way this industry is a bit like a drug and I do have an addictive personality. Coffee is my drug of choice, and music is definitely another, but my ultimate addiction is my kids.

Outside our house in Australia in
1999. From left to right: Mike,
Andrew, me, Chris and Danny.

I needed to plan how I was going to get back into the music industry, so after the stint in the US I went back to the resort on Bribie Island. By this time I had invested in a lot of properties, including the resort. Mum and Dad had been working really hard and needed some time to themselves, and I went out to give them a break with my brother. So I went from a pop star who sold out Wembley Arena, via a psychiatric hospital, to being a receptionist/waiter/cleaner! I did a bit of everything on the resort before handing it back over to my parents and moving to Cyprus, where Mum and Dad had an apartment. I bought some land, and together with my brother Mike and my sister Debbie, we bought a gym. Mike and I ran the gym and Debbie set up shop in a beauty salon downstairs. It felt good to be doing a proper job and mixing with people – it was satisfying. I was finally getting my head straight, sorting myself out. The time out of the limelight was exactly what I needed. To have everything and then lose it was tough on me but I was lucky, I bounced back. Some people don't.

Owning the gym meant that I started to get fit and tone up again, but I was careful not to let my body obsession take over this time. I was always quite vain from a young age. I hated my nose and wanted to change it and I actually had a nose job in 1998. Apart from these early shots that no one has ever seen before, you won't find pictures of my old nose because I have scrapped them! At the time I would never allow a single shot to be taken side-on. I'd move cameras and chairs in interviews so that you couldn't see the hook, as I called it. Remarkably the press didn't find out about it. Luckily the surgeon didn't have to break my nose and the bruising went down really quickly so no one noticed anything. It was only years later that I owned up to it! I have had some Botox, once just before the wedding and again last January because I started to notice crow's feet around my eyes. Despite the rumours that I have fake pecs in the 'Mysterious Girl' video I can categorically say that I didn't.

As part of my plan to get back into the music business, I knew I needed to get Claire to manage me again. I nagged her for eighteen months before she agreed to take me back on – I remember we met at Café Rouge in Victoria Station to sign the contracts. My mum, my dad, my brother and my sister were all there as well. My dad wanted to be sure that I'd be looked after. After everything I'd been through, he wanted to be sure that it would never happen again, that I was protected. He and Claire are very close and he has always trusted her, as do I, with my life. A horrible chapter of my life had come to an end. Fame had got to me and royally screwed me over. I will never let that happen again.

I'M A CELEBRITY... GET ME OUT OF HERE!

IN THE FIRST SIX MONTHS OF RE-SIGNING WITH CLAIRE WE RECEIVED SEVERAL OFFERS FOR ME TO TAKE PART IN REALITY SHOWS, INCLUDING CELEBRITY BIG BROTHER, BUT IT WASN'T UNTIL I HEARD ABOUT *I'M A CELEBRITY . . . GET ME OUT OF HERE!* THAT I THOUGHT, 'YEAH, THIS IS SOMETHING I'D LIKE TO DO.' Claire had explained that it was a bit like a mix of two other shows, *Survivor* and *Fear Factor*, each of which had a challenge element to them. And it was that which I liked the sound of. I'd been in the gym, so I knew I was toned up and physically ready for a challenge – the idea even excited me. You see, there's one thing that I've always been frightened of, and one thing that I knew there'd be a lot of in the show . . . spiders.

My biggest fear is huntsman spiders. If you haven't been to Australia you won't understand this, so let me explain: they're the size of your hand; they're nomadic so they often wander into your home; and, to top it all, they jump. Even the name is scary – a 'hunting man', a man-hunting spider – you might as well call them Mike Tyson or The Terminator. Almost every night in the summertime you'll see one of these things, somewhere, and go white as a ghost. Growing up I would lie in bed at night, freaking out, leaving just enough space under the duvet for my nose to breathe, scared to go to sleep and wake up to find one of them sitting on my face . . . So when I went into the jungle, one of the reasons was to face that fear head on. I thought, 'If you're ever going to do it, do it now. No amount of therapy is ever going to do as good a job as this.'

So we got the ball rolling and I met up with the people from ITV. In my interview I thought I'd be clever and use a bit of reverse psychology. They asked me what my biggest fear was and I said, 'Snakes – definitely snakes. Can't stand 'em.' That was rubbish, snakes don't bother me at all – when you live in Australia with nine of the ten deadliest types of snake you'd think I'd be petrified of them, but I wasn't. So I figured that although I was bound to come across some spiders – we were going to be in the jungle, after all – I had probably reduced the chances of them really going overboard on the spider front. Little did I know!

'A LOT OF PEOPLE ASK ME IF IT WAS LOVE AT FIRST SIGHT WHEN I MET KATIE, BUT IT WASN'T. THERE WAS NO IMMEDIATE EYES-LOCKING-ACROSS-A-CROWDED-ROOM SITUATION BETWEEN US.'

Soon the day came and we headed off to the hotel to meet the other contestants. We were staying on the Gold Coast at the Palazzo Versace, which is beautiful. My friend owns it so I got looked after really well. That first day I met Katie Price, or Jordan as she was known at the time. I was told that she was a Page Three model. I didn't know anything about her, given that I'd been out of the country for so long – I'd only seen a picture of her three days before we finally met. I remember my exact words on seeing the photo: 'She's pretty, she's got a great body, but she's not my type.' Both Claire and Mike told me in no uncertain terms to stay away from her, and Mike warned me, 'Pete, whatever you do, don't flirt.' I said, 'Look, you've got no worries about that, I'm not interested, I just want to get through the trials.' He also warned me against singing on camera, saying I'd look like an idiot. He was right and needless to say I didn't take either bit of his advice – something I have since lived to regret to some extent, for obvious reasons.

A lot of people ask me if it was love at first sight when I met Katie, but it wasn't. There was no immediate eyes-locking-across-a-crowded-room situation between us. She did tell me later that she knew immediately and that she was attracted to me from the first moment, even before we started talking. (She had had her cards read before going

to Australia and they had predicted everything, apparently – that she would fall in love and meet the one she was going to marry. Because of that she said she felt a nervousness that she'd never felt before. It was full-on stuff!) But, for me, Katie was not an obvious choice because all the women I'd ever gone out with before were very, very different to her. I've always gone for dark-skinned, dark-haired ladies – not a supposedly feisty blonde with big boobs and a penchant for surgery. Far from it, in fact. Initially, in fairness to her, Katie actually seemed pretty shy. After everything I'd been told, I was expecting someone to make her entrance wearing a miniskirt. So when Katie walked in wearing jeans, heels and a nice polo-neck jumper I was taken aback. She had her hair in braids, and I remember being struck by her green eyes and lack of make-up. She didn't need any: I remember thinking, 'Wow, she's a really pretty girl.' At first she wouldn't look me in the eye, and there was a vulnerability about her that intrigued me. She wasn't at all what I was expecting.

On the first night, all the contestants got together in the evening for dinner. If you watch the programme you might imagine that everyone meets for the first time in the jungle, but you don't; you have a few days to get to know one another beforehand. At dinner Katie was there with her mum, Amy, and her baby son, Harvey. Seeing her with Harvey was another thing that drew me towards her, and as the banter between us got going I started thinking, 'She's a really cool girl.' It was hard to talk too much as the music was getting really loud and there was a disco going on too – I did a bit of karaoke, which helped get things going! The next night a few people came to my parents' house for a steak – they live just fifteen minutes from the hotel. Neil 'Razor' Ruddock, Kerry Katona, Mike Read, Diane Modahl and a few others came over for my dad's mean T-bone steak. In the days leading up to entering the jungle the show sent us all to the zoo, and it was then that Katie and I started to flirt. It was already too late to stop what was between us before we even got into the jungle. Although Claire wasn't keen on Jordan's reputation or what she'd read about her in the newspapers, I hadn't heard of Jordan before and I knew nothing about her. They were saying she was a bit of man-eater but when you first meet Katie that doesn't come across at all. I had better explain now so that you understand: the woman I met in the jungle was Katie Price. I never called Katie by the name 'Jordan' throughout our relationship. At that point, even though we were flirting, I never thought for one moment anything would really happen between us properly. I didn't want to come on to her and look bad on camera, like someone sleazy, but there was something that got me interested – a power thing, maybe – that even now I can't put my finger on.

THE I'M A CELEBRITY ... GANG OF 2004. FROM LEFT TO RIGHT: LORD BROCKET, ALEX BEST, KERRY KATONA, ME, MIKE READ, DIANE MODAHL, KATIE WITH HARVEY, NEIL RUDDOCK AND JENNIE BOND.

On the day of the first programme, all the contestants were woken at 2 a.m. and given a massive breakfast to try to set us up for what lay ahead: our entry into the jungle. I couldn't even look at my food. I felt terrible. Claire was urging me to have something because she knew that I wasn't going to be eating for a while, but I couldn't get anything down. I was really nervous. The pictures taken as we went in don't really do justice to how I was feeling, because I felt sick to my stomach. I managed to get the coffee down my neck, but that was it. I was more concerned with getting in there and getting on with it. My hair is naturally quite curly, which I'm not a big fan of, and being on the TV for the first time in ages I wanted to look okay. I also had someone I was flirting with and I didn't want to let myself down on the hair front, so . . . I wrapped some hair wax in cling film and stuck it between my bum cheeks! Even when I was frisked by the guard as I went in they didn't find it. While everyone else was trying to smuggle something sensible in, I was smuggling in goods for my hair . . . mad! That just about says it all. (In complete contrast, I did a shoot with *Heat* magazine last year and they wanted to make me look different, so they stripped me back – in more ways than one! – and made me lose the gel. I couldn't believe how much I liked it. I really thought I was going to hate it: my security blanket was gone, it was like I was bare. But I looked just like my son Junior – the similarity was uncanny and I really liked it. In the past I didn't get much say because Katie wanted my hair spiky, she liked me looking like someone out of a boy band. Now I keep toying with the idea of losing the gel completely, but I'm worried that I won't be able to recreate the look again. I'm going to have to practise though, because it would take me a lot less time to get ready in the morning!)

THIS IS AN IMAGE FROM THE *HEAT* SHOOT THAT
SHOWS WHAT I LOOK LIKE WITHOUT LOADS OF
HAIR GEL. I LOOK JUST LIKE JUNIOR!

Katie's behaviour really confused me. On the one hand she was flirting with me and on the other she'd play it cool, flirting as well with other people in the camp. She would never come over to me and sit with me; she would always be sitting on Razor's lap or sitting next to Brocket. It made me question what was really going on, if anything, between us. I liked the banter between us, and most of the time I took her put-downs as a compliment. Weird as that sounds, I knew she was trying to get my attention. When she commented that my lower abs could do with a bit of work it stung, but it also attracted me to her. When the cameras weren't on us she would whisper much nicer words in my ears. All this played on my mind and when everyone was asleep at night, I would lie awake thinking, wondering what was actually happening. I eventually

questioned her about it and asked her why she was like that, but she just looked at me as if I was mad, like I was imagining it. It was starting to drive me insane, never knowing where I stood with her. People in the camp were commenting about the chemistry between us, but it was Lord Brocket who thought he saw another side to what was happening. He took me aside and said, 'My boy, you're such a nice man, and I'm sad to have to tell you, but you're being played. She's playing you.' I'd say, 'No, no, she's not,' but towards the end, when he explained that she'd asked him to set her up with one of his friends, I started to worry that he might be right. What was I meant to do? I was already in deep.

Hunger pains didn't help my state of mind either. They were so bad you didn't know what you were imagining and what was real. As a viewer you might think that we can't really survive on so little, but we genuinely do. Less than it appears, in fact. Beans and just two tablespoons of rice a day. Even the water had to be treated before you could drink it: you have to boil it and then leave it overnight to settle – it's a right palaver. When you wash yourself you end up with leeches on your body when you've finished! Half of these things the viewers never get to see. So I was always starving: I'd never experienced hunger pains like it before. Starving hungry and with feelings for a girl that I hadn't expected equalled a very confused Mr Andre! As well as the hunger pangs and my confused emotions, there were the insects that we had to contend with in the jungle. Despite my attempts at being clever, the crew knew before they even met me that I was terrified of spiders, so for my Bushtucker Trial they really went to town . . . I had to put my head in a Perspex box while they unleashed a heap of wildlife in there with me. Just the smell was horrendous. The first box was full of grubs and not too bad, but they got progressively worse and eventually we came to the box containing those huntsman spiders I so dreaded. I had to collect a star using my teeth. A star with a massive huntsman spider sat on it, looking me straight in the eyes. As if things couldn't get worse, the final challenge was to lie in a Perspex coffin filled with spiders – jumping spiders, wolf spiders, huntsman . . . every type of spider you could think of. When I finally got into the coffin and they shut the lid, locking it, I thought things were as bad as they could get. So much for that . . . I shouted, 'Ready!' and found sixty thousand cockroaches promptly poured over me. Yep. All over me. With spiders jumping all over them. And then I had to start the trial. Somehow I managed to complete it and collect all ten stars, and I put it completely down to hunger. Starvation will make you do things you didn't believe yourself capable of. And for a guy like me who likes his food, it's a killer!

Looking back, there's a lot about the experience that I feel proud of. It was just two weeks, but it changed my life for ever. Two years ago I revisited the *I'm a Celebrity . . .* jungle. I drove from my parents' house and met up with Dr Bob, the guy that oversees all the Bushtucker Trials. It was such a unique experience spending time in the outback that going back like this was quite moving. All the memories I had from my time in there came flooding back. They let us trek through so that we could see the old camp, but we couldn't actually go in, which was a bit of a shame. The memories were there, though, and I could almost smell the campfire again. For me, being in the jungle was a purifying experience; it cleanses you and puts things into perspective, probably because you are back to basics.

... espite my niggling doubts about everything I'd witnessed during the show, I had completely fallen for Katie Price. We were in an intense relationship the day we walked out of that jungle – we didn't really spend any time apart. We wanted to work out our feelings for one another before parading the relationship in front of the press. Unbeknownst to us, while we were in the jungle, Katie's mother had asked Claire if she'd take on Katie as a client too, because she wanted a change of management to get away from her past career as a topless model. Claire accepted on that basis knowing that she could make Katie more well known. When we got out, Katie got Claire to sort both our itineraries so that they matched and we wouldn't be apart – that was part of the deal. She wanted to be with me constantly, to avoid any stories claiming that our romance was off or anything untoward.

It was massively full-on and although we tried to stay out of the media initially, people wanted to know what was going on between us. It upsets me that allegations have been made that Kate and I were told what we could and couldn't do, because that's just not true. The decision to stay out of the spotlight for a while was ours, as I say, so that we could see how we felt about one another outside the jungle, in the real world. I don't think I truly believed that Katie felt the way I felt, loved me the way I loved her. I kept asking why she would fancy me and have this instant love for me – I was wary of that. But ultimately we were obsessed with each other. I thought I had found the real Katie Price under the Jordan façade. Despite her offish way in the jungle, when we were out Katie wanted everyone to know that we were in love. After the end-of-show party she came up to my room in the hotel and in front of my brother Danny she asked me to marry her. I thought she was joking and when she finally left my room after begging me to let her stay my mind was all over the place once more. I couldn't believe what had happened. In the space of three days she asked me to marry her thirty times, and she continued to ask every day after that for four months.

As you can probably tell, when I look back at how it was at the beginning of our relationship, I have very mixed feelings. There's no denying that at that time Katie was everything to me and I would have walked over hot coals for her. There was nothing I could do about it. She seemed sweet, she had a vulnerability about her that it seemed no one had ever seen before *I'm a Celebrity* . . . and I think she surprised everyone with her gutsy behaviour. She had my heart pretty quickly, and when we were in the jungle my feelings got stronger and stronger towards her, particularly in the lead-up to those trials when I began to feel very protective of her. Looking back at the pictures of us together in the jungle doesn't bring up unhappy memories, just memories that are a part of my history. I was madly in love. I was enjoying myself and I had never expected to feel like that.

Falling in love on *I'm a Celebrity . . .* was an experience. It's not something I want to either condemn or condone. I don't have to, because everything in life happens for a reason. I was meant to go on that show and I was meant to fall in love. I'm a great believer in fate. I had an amazing experience in the jungle and have made some lifelong friends. I still keep in touch with Jennie Bond and Mike Read – we chat on the phone and text each other occasionally to see how things are. They have both offered me a massive amount of support since things went wrong with my marriage.

Katie is the mother of my children. I suppose I could really put the boot in, but I'm not going to – it ended in tears, but I have beautiful children who mean everything to me. I need to be truthful in my account of how I felt at the time, despite it being very different to how I see it now. Because she is the mother of my children I will always care for her, but I can't lie and say it's easy on a day-to-day basis, because it's not. Far from it. We don't see eye to eye on a lot of things. Our relationship now is not as amicable as I'd like it to be and as it could be, but for the children I must continue trying.

Someone said to me once that when things get you down, you have to think, is this going to matter to me in a year's time? With most situations you know it's not going to, and that puts whatever's going on into perspective. You have to think, 'Do I remember exactly how I felt a year ago, and is that relevant now?' The answer is probably no. Draw on the experiences good and bad that you've had and use them to move forward. So I'm moving on now and things don't hurt me quite the way they used to – I have built a barrier and it's hard for anyone to get at me through it.

WELCOME BACK TO THE MADNESS

MY WORK WAS REALLY BUSY. THE STINT ON *I'M A CELEBRITY . . .* HAD LAUNCHED ME BACK INTO THE MEDIA SPOTLIGHT. As soon as I walked over the bridge and left the jungle, Claire was waiting for me. She was so excited and happy for me that she had tears in her eyes. Great things were in the pipeline. I had a new album deal, a UK tour and there was even a calendar. My record company wanted to re-release 'Mysterious Girl'. Wow! Work was rolling in. All this was strange because I'd been out of the limelight for so long and all the media interviews seemed like something straight from my past. I couldn't believe this had happened in just a few short weeks. I'd desperately wanted a second chance and here it was being given to me – I didn't want to mess it up.

The re-release of 'Mysterious Girl' was amazing: third time lucky, because it went to number one. It's in the Guinness Book of World Records for the number of times it was released before finally hitting the top spot. It's incredible that this song became so popular. When it was first released in 1995 it only made number forty-five in the charts and people didn't seem to like it at all. After The Box started to play the video it climbed up the video charts and they urged us to re-release it. Eventually we did and the single went straight in at number three, where it stayed for six weeks. The third time is the one I think most people remember. Radio 1 DJ Chris Moyles got behind me when I was in the jungle in 2004. He campaigned for me to release 'Mysterious Girl' again, and when I did, it hit the jackpot. Three attempts and it got there! We used the same video, filmed on the beautiful Phi Phi Island, Thailand, but this time round everyone loved it! I gave proceeds of the re-release to the NSPCC, and later became an ambassador for them, which is a huge honour.

Following the success of 'Mysterious Girl', I released the album *The Long Road Back*, which included two versions of the track – a radio edit and the version that had finally hit the top spot. It was a fun album, but it included the song 'Insania' – a track that continues to haunt me. I have nightmares about it! If ever I do a TV interview, guess which video is dragged out? Yep, you got it – 'Insania'. How embarrassing. At the time I wasn't keen to have it released. I wanted to start afresh and become a credible songwriter and musician, but 'Insania' was what people wanted. It's the hit I love to hate and was a nightmare from the very beginning. We did a shoot in Spain for the video and it rained the entire time. I remember being disappointed in the whole thing. I'd wanted something more like a Jamiroquai video, but that's not how it came out. As I say, all a bit of a nightmare. It was my fault for not listening to my brother's advice before I went into the jungle and singing my way through the weeks I was in there. Now I have that song to remind me that Mike was right! Anyway, it sold – whether you liked it or hated it (like me), it was a winner. It debuted at number three in the UK charts to be precise, which secured me my seventh Top Five UK hit. I couldn't complain because my music career was back on track.

'FOR ME THE 'INSANIA' TOUR WAS ABOUT SHOWING THAT I COULD DANCE AS WELL AS SING, THAT I HAD THE WHOLE PACKAGE.'

THIS PAGE AND NEXT: THE 'INSANIA' TOUR

I n one way, *The Long Road Back* was my musical comeback, but in another it wasn't, because it was never about me being taken seriously as an artist, which I've always desperately craved. I can write music, I can sing and I've always wanted to be considered a credible artist but once you've done cheesy, it's hard to get away from that image. I have had a fair amount of criticism over the years from the press and some harsh critics but I hope that my recent work shows what I can really do. I want to be accepted as an artist, but it's hard work and I know that I have a lot to prove.

In 2004 I got to tour again – touring is something I absolutely adore. It was the summer after I left the jungle and the first time in ages that I'd been able to showcase my talents. I wanted it to be incredible. I always want to make sure I put on the best show possible, that people will enjoy every minute. For me, the 'Insania' tour was about showing that I could dance as well as sing, that I had the whole package. As always, I felt like I had something to prove and I wanted people to see that I could do it all. I still had a bit of the American influence going on – although my clothes were a lot less baggy. (Poor Claire used to have to do a massive shop for me whenever we were in the US because I loved that style so much!) I still had the shiny outfits so I looked bright and young, but I was moving away from the look I'd had in the 1990s.

Katie came with me on tour with Harvey for almost a whole month – she wasn't about to let me go anywhere on my own in case we were pictured apart and a false story emerged. Harvey absolutely loved the shows, just like Junior and Tiaamii loved my 'Revelation' tour. Although I sometimes felt tugged in two directions, by the demands of work and the demands of our new relationship, I was happy. I was with a woman I loved and I had taken to Harvey, big time. He is a gorgeous boy who I love very much. I never found the idea of taking him on daunting – from the moment I saw him I thought he was the most adorable kid in the world. The bond between us developed naturally. As soon as he could speak, he called me Dad. The first time he uttered that word I had a smile on my face for about a week! He was and always will be like my own child to me, and I love him every bit as much. Since the split I do still get to see him, although I'd like to see him more. For the moment I'm not able to, but appreciate the time I have with him. Harvey has grown up a lot recently and is really well behaved. He's so loving to his brother and sister, it's a joy to see. Being with Harvey before Junior was born gave me a chance to learn a bit about being a father – something I sing about in the song 'Unconditional' on *Revelation*, a song that means a lot to me. I have pictures all over my houses in Brighton and Cyprus of Harvey – big canvases so that he is always near to me – and I hope that he will always be allowed to be a part of my family and my life.

Touring meant that I was in my element, back doing what I loved . . . performing in front of an audience. It was quite a nostalgic experience really – it'd been years since I'd been being screamed at by fans and had that amazing warm feeling that performing on stage in front of thousands of people gives you. It's like another world that you're transported to when you're up there on the stage: you're in a dreamworld, a bubble, and no one can touch you. Performing is like a drug, it's addictive. At every show there was mass hysteria – lots of audience interaction and me being thrown out to the crowds, which I loved. The fans seemed to be getting younger! (On my latest tour I've made sure that audience interaction is a big part – except a lot more grown-up this time!) At that point, things seemed to be going well for me, both personally and professionally.

DISNEY CHANNEL KIDS AWARDS, THE ROYAL ALBERT HALL, SEPTEMBER 2004

WITH MY BROTHERS MIKE,
CHRIS AND ANDREW

THE WEDDING CIRCUS

I HAVE ALWAYS WANTED TO HAVE A MARRIAGE LIKE MY PARENTS HAVE. A MARRIAGE THAT LASTS FOR EVER, THROUGH THICK AND THIN, LOVE CONQUERS ALL . . . THAT SORT OF THING. Although I've been burned I still believe that is possible: my mum and dad are proof that if you love one another and you persevere through the hard patches then your marriage can stand the test of time. I have failed spectacularly on that front and it's not something I'm happy about or proud of. For me, getting married and having kids is the ultimate achievement – to think my children would end up being from a broken home really upsets me. One day my children will read the old newspapers and magazines and I hope that when they see I haven't sold out they will be proud, and know that I always tried to do the right thing. I feel very strongly about that. They are still so young, it's hard for them to understand what's going on at the moment, but one day they will understand and I want them to know then that I have always put them first, that they are my priority. When the kids are with me I put away the magazines and papers so they can't see them. I just want to protect them.

Until Katie, no one had snared me. I was a young lad when I hit the big time first time around so, without wanting to sound big-headed, it's not like I've been short of offers. There was really only one other girl I considered marrying – Laura Vasquez. We met years ago, as Laura has always been friends with my sister, Debbie, and we became close friends ourselves for a long time. During that time we always wanted to be together, but we never did anything, never crossed the line between friends and lovers. We cared for each other and I always said she was the one I'd end up marrying. But we both knew that it had to be all or nothing. She said, 'You keep telling me, "One day, one day, one day . . ." but "one day" never happens. So, are you ready?' And I wasn't. Eventually she'd had enough. And when I finally came to a point in my life where I wanted to settle down she was with someone. Now she is happily married with two kids, and is still good friends with my sister and my cousin, and I'm happy for her. I will always look at her with respect. She will always be a wonderful person and will remain someone I hold in high regard.

I don't know what it was about Katie that was different to all the other girls I'd been out with, but our relationship was moving at a hundred miles an hour and when she fell pregnant with Junior so quickly it was quite a shock for me. We did so many tests: we couldn't believe it. We probably should have waited a bit longer but I was so excitable and it was all so quick and mad and crazy. Anyway, you can't regret things like that – just look at the wonderful children that I have. So it was time to grow up, time to be a man. I was already learning the ropes with Harvey, and now it was time to be a biological dad for the first time.

The only person we told about the baby was my brother Mike – Katie didn't want anyone to know. She was adamant and she made that very clear to me – we'd tell the world, or rather she'd tell the media, when she was ready for it. I wanted to shout about it I was so excited, but until she was ready for us to tell people she wanted me to keep my mouth shut. I have to say, it was difficult to keep a secret like that. Because nobody apart from Mike knew about the pregnancy we were under even more pressure than usual. (We didn't even tell Claire until Katie was nearly five months gone! She was competing in the Eurovision Song Contest, wearing this pink Lycra outfit that showed every lump and bump, and as soon as Claire knew Katie was pregnant she warned her not to do it. But she did, and the cat was very quickly out of the bag then.)

IN MAY 2005, WE ATTENDED THE *HOUSE OF WAX* UK FILM PREMIERE AT THE VUE CINEMA IN LONDON'S LEICESTER SQUARE

ON HOLIDAY IN TENERIFE,
KATIE WAS SEVEN MONTHS
PREGNANT

RIGHT: I HAVE A PASSION FOR CARS,
I ALWAYS HAVE DONE. THE FIRST CAR
I FELL IN LOVE WITH WAS A FERRARI — I
NAMED IT THE STALLION

The wedding wheels were put rapidly into motion, and we set a date for the following year. By that point our reality show was doing really well and cameras were following us around everywhere. You'll see from the footage that Katie did a lot of the deciding – as always, she knew exactly what she wanted. I was in love, so, perhaps foolishly, I let her get on with it.

Katie had a hen-do but, for me, there was no stag-do – Katie didn't want me to have one. She begged me not to because she didn't trust me one hundred per cent. She thought I'd have a stripper or that I'd get up to something, which of course would never have happened . . . She made it clear that if there was even a picture of a girl with her arm around me, or just next to me, the marriage would be off. So it was a choice between having a stag-do or a marriage. At that stage I'd made my choices and I believe that if you make your bed, you lie in it, but I think it's weird to have been in that predicament in the first place. Being stopped from having a stag-do doesn't say much about trust.

We got married three months after Junior was born, in September 2005. Katie was the kind of woman who was, like, 'Why wait? Let's do it now!' and I admired her for that; I thought that was cool. And after all, she was the first girl I ever got pregnant, the first girl I ever got engaged to, and the first girl I ever married. I grew up believing you don't have kids out of wedlock – accidents happen, but it's not a situation you should go looking for. So once I'd decided that we were going ahead with it, that was it. Barriers came down, this was love, this was going to be for ever . . . My parents have been together for fifty-five years, and we come from a family that believes in marriage as everlasting. Only under extreme circumstances would you walk away. And I've always stuck by that. People say weddings are stressful but mine wasn't. I was in love. I was making the commitment of a lifetime.

> 'IN MANY WAYS, LOOKING BACK, WHAT KATIE AND I HAD WAS CRAZY LOVE, BUT WHEN I GOT MARRIED I MARRIED FOR LOVE, I MARRIED FOR LIFE.'

The actual wedding was a pretty flashy day – many would say tacky. But it was a magical day, and when I took those vows I meant every word. Katie wanted everything to be pink and on that front I did put my foot down a bit. I wanted it to be slightly masculine too. If I am ever to marry again (and I think that's a long way off) things will be very different. I am an easygoing guy but I'd like a little more say in the planning, and something not so showy. I'm not particularly flash – I've got things like nice cars but I'll have the windows blacked out so I can enjoy the car without anyone knowing it is me. (I have a passion for cars. I always have done and I was very proud with our first Ferrari – I named it The Stallion. I don't have it any more but I have a Bentley GT convertible and a 4x4 Porsche Carrera. One day I'd like to get a Lamborghini – I've always loved them but I have to try to remember that cars are a liability, not an investment!)

Two weeks later we went on our honeymoon to the Maldives. It was incredible. I called it the 'moneymoon' because we had agreed to film the first four days as part of a deal with ITV, after which we'd have the honeymoon. Looking back, it was a bit of a weird thing to do, but the 'moneymoon' soon gave way to the proper honeymoon and our well-deserved break. Kate's mum also came along, which again was a bit strange, but that was okay – I didn't have a problem with that, and it was great to have Harvey and JJ with us too. Overall we had an amazing time and I have great memories of it. The Maldives really is the most picturesque place you can imagine, with the most beautiful weather. We swam, sunbathed and just relaxed. And the hotel . . . The villa was crazy – it had a revolving bed so that you could look at the ocean any time you wanted, a massive wet room, a glass floor in the lounge so that you could see the stingrays swimming underneath. I even had my own coffee machine so I could wake up in the morning with a nice cup of coffee! It was the trip of a lifetime.

In many ways, looking back, what Katie and I had was crazy love, but when I got married I married for love, I married for life.

October 2005, us at the National TV Awards, Royal Albert Hall, London

THINGS CAN ONLY GET BETTER... CAN'T THEY?

JUNIOR (OR JJ, AS I CALL HIM) WAS BORN ON 13 JUNE 2005 AT 10:13 A.M. I DIDN'T STOP CRYING AFTERWARDS, I WAS SO HAPPY. IT'S AN EXPERIENCE YOU CAN'T EXPLAIN OR DO JUSTICE TO WHEN YOU PUT IT INTO WORDS. I WAS THERE FOR THE BIRTH ITSELF. Although Katie wanted to have a natural birth it proved impossible and she was given a caesarean section. We were in hospital for five days and I didn't leave her side the whole time. There was nowhere else I wanted to be. It was a magical experience. I believe that sometimes emotions are unlocked at different times, by certain events. For instance, if someone passes away, a feeling of mourning is unlocked that you would never have experienced otherwise. I've experienced love and I've experienced happiness, but the feeling that was unlocked the moment I saw my baby boy was saved for that moment. I could never, ever explain that feeling – that love, that joy. Words will never explain the happiness, the crying and the laughter. It was as if God had said, 'Here's the key to unlock that emotion,' and just handed it to me. I felt exactly the same when Princess was born, but the first time is something you'll never forget. I could have died right there and I would have been in heaven. It's probably one of the reasons why I'm so close to my kids. There was love there already though. Harvey had taught me how to be a dad before I had JJ, and my love for him is unconditional, it's a thank-you love – because he taught me.

It is Greek tradition to name your son after your father or the bride's father, and your daughter after your mother or the bride's mother. Before Junior was born we had big rows about names because Katie wasn't keen on my father's name, Savva (Greek for Sabbath). We had agreed on the name Daniel because it was Katie's brother's name and my brother's name. Eventually I suggested Junior, a name I really like, and we agreed on Savva for the middle name.

The pregnancy hadn't been an easy one and afterwards Katie suffered terribly with post-natal depression, something that wasn't diagnosed for quite some time. In the early days Katie was guiding me on what to do and how to do it because she'd already gone through it all with Harvey as a baby, but we'd row about how Junior should be brought up and the depression meant that she'd blame me for things that weren't necessarily my fault, which was difficult. Our relationship was still okay, but I knew it was down to me to try to hold things together. I'm not sure I really understood what was going on, but I knew something was wrong, even though Kate wouldn't admit to it and said she was fine. She was hard to live with at that time.

I was thrown into fatherhood with a bang as it became more apparent over time that there was a problem with Katie bonding with Junior. Katie seemed unable to be close with the baby and I needed to fill that gap. I found that very difficult to deal with or to understand, but it has meant that JJ and I developed a special bond: we are very, very close even now, and he is never far away from me.

Junior is an incredibly tactile, happy child who loves to cuddle. He doesn't really understand that Mummy and Daddy have split up but he knows he has two bedrooms now. He also knows that his mummy has remarried – I just don't think he understands it fully yet, but he will come to me and ask me questions. Whenever he does, I do my best to try to answer as honestly as I can. But because he's a child, he's my baby, it's very difficult. Family values have always been very important to me, and like my parents I would do anything for my children. My heart breaks to see them suffer. I often find myself having to walk out of the room as my eyes well up with sadness at how things have turned out. Children are very savvy and catch on to things so quickly and unfortunately they do see things I would prefer they didn't. As far as possible, I want to protect their naivety. I have already said that I hope I never have to give the reason why I left Katie; it would be too upsetting for the kids and unless I'm forced to I would rather not.

Like anyone else, there are some things in my life that I would repeat but there are others I'd rather forget. The last few years have been hugely up and down for me, both professionally and personally, and one of the worst periods was when I contracted meningitis. To be so ill like that and recover makes you grateful for everything you have. I've learned not to take things for granted. Life is precious, and when you've been close to the other side it puts things into perspective.

It all started after a meal we had in Los Angeles. It was May 2007 and we were in the US for the launch of our show, *Katie and Peter: Stateside*, which was going out on E!. We had to do a load of interviews for radio stations and for magazines like *People* and *US Weekly*. It was a really big deal because we wanted the show to go down well with the American audience and so we needed to promote it quite heavily. We were out there for ten days and rented this incredible, ultra-modern house in Beverly Hills that was set into a rock, literally built into the rock face! It was so big that the film crew, stylist, make-up, our management and Kate and I could all stay in it together – it was like the Big Brother house. Kate was pregnant with Tiaamii at the time and Claire was pregnant with her son Nysna so it was pretty full-on for them, but we had a really great trip and lots of laughs. Any time off that we had, we would go and visit the attractions like Universal Studios, which I absolutely loved, and we were able to let off steam after all the work we were doing. In the evenings we would mostly eat out but sometimes we'd order takeaways and eat in, and would all congregate around the massive dining-room table. It was around that very table that we had a meal that led to one of the most horrific experiences I have ever had. We had a fast-food takeaway and although everyone ate the same only I started to feel poorly afterwards. I went to bed that night feeling really strange. I woke up every few hours tasting oil from the fried food and had a really weird sensation I had never felt before. At first, I thought that I must have a bit of food poisoning . . .

By the morning I knew something was really wrong. I didn't know what, I couldn't put my finger on it, but I knew something was up. I think everyone around me just thought I was having a bit of an off day, a lazy day, but it wasn't that at all. Katie was saying, 'Look, if you can't be bothered to come shopping with us, just say.' But I wasn't well. I felt terrible and I wasn't getting any better. When everyone came back from shopping we had to pack up because we were leaving LA. I felt weak and was finding it hard to do anything. It was at that point that I said, 'There is something really wrong with my body.' They all just thought I had 'man flu' and kept telling me to get on with it.

threw up the whole flight back to the UK! We ended up on a Virgin Atlantic flight with Matt Damon, and Claire got to sit right next to him. She was joking that she had finally got to spend a night with Matt Damon because all they had between them was a Virgin screen . . . as she said it I got up and ran to the toilets, and stayed there for the whole flight, vomiting. When we got back on terra firma I had to see the doctor at the airport was so bad. I think everyone was beginning to realize that I wasn't actually having a bout of man flu but that I really wasn't very well. As time went on the sickness was subsiding but it felt as though I'd been hit on the back of the head with a hammer. I was experiencing pain I'd never felt before. Eventually I called a doctor again, who came out to the house and diagnosed me with a virus; she said I'd be fine. But then she had to come out again, and said that if things didn't get better I should call an ambulance

That night I changed the sheets on the bed three times – they were soaked through and so was I. I kept saying to Katie, 'Something is wrong, something is wrong, I know it.' The next morning that was it. I felt terrible and I was convinced there was something the matter with me so I said, 'I'm calling an ambulance.' Katie said, 'You can't call the ambulance for a flu.' Of course she was right, for the flu you wouldn't and if I'd thought she had the flu and was about to call an ambulance I would have said the same thing to her, but I knew in my heart that this wasn't the flu, that something was wrong with me, big time. I kept begging, 'Please get an ambulance, something isn't right.' I was relieved when an ambulance turned up and took me to the hospital.

was taken to the hospital but because it was so busy I had to stay in A & E for two days because there wasn't a bed on a ward for me. There was no privacy at all, it was just a room off A & E; it was horrible. Claire tried everything to get me a room but I was so ill they wouldn't let me be moved, and they wanted to be sure I wasn't carrying a disease had no choice: I had to stay where I was. They put me on a drip and did some tests but they couldn't find out what was wrong with me. I was deteriorating quickly and after three days they had to do a lumbar puncture; basically putting a needle in my spine. The pain was horrendous – I can only imagine that's what childbirth is like! I was so weak and tears were rolling down my cheeks. Eventually they established that I had meningitis. The doctor said to me, 'We have a bit of a problem: you have meningitis but we're not sure of the strain – it could be viral or bacterial. One of them is deadly and one of them isn't.' As soon as I heard that I started applying The Secret. I said to myself, over and over, 'I am going to be fine and I am going to walk out of here in two weeks.'

CAN ONLY GET BETTER . . . CAN'T THEY?

The news spread like wildfire. On the cover of the newspapers they were reporting that I had a brain bug. At that stage even I didn't know how serious things were. A brain bug sounded terrible and it started to play on my mind. I was really worried. Katie had work commitments, so she was with me as often as she could, but it wasn't easy. My mum flew over from Cyprus to be with me as soon as she heard the news and my sister came as well. Unfortunately my dad was too poorly to travel at the time and although it was nothing life-threatening he couldn't be there. He was devastated when he found out what I'd been diagnosed with. He only knew of one other person who had had meningitis and that person had died, so it was his worst fear. The reports in the papers saying I was dying obviously didn't help and it was really scary for all of us. But although it was frightening, I was also overwhelmed with the amount of support I got. The office was inundated with calls, people sent me flowers and chocolates, and Jonathan Ross sent me a pile of porn to look at, which made me laugh! Seriously, the support I got was incredible– I couldn't believe it, it was lovely.

The doctors told me that they didn't know how long I'd be in hospital for and that it could be very serious. I was hooked up to drips, I was losing weight rapidly yet all I kept thinking was, 'I am going to be out of here in two weeks.' I was so weak and while a part of me thought that I was going to die, the other part wouldn't let me believe it. I don't know how and I don't know why, but somehow I knew I was going to get out, that I was going to be okay. I really believed that. I visualized myself leaving the hospital wearing white (don't ask me why!) and sure enough, when I walked out of there two weeks later, defying the odds, I was wearing white three-quarter-length shorts, a white T-shirt and a white cap. I'd done it; I'd walked out. I struggled, but I walked out.

The doctors at East Surrey hospital were amazing to me, and everyone there really looked after me. They said it was a miracle that I'd recovered so well, but that for ten weeks I wouldn't be able to do anything much at all. Two weeks later I was training again. I swear The Secret works; you just have to believe. I'm very lucky that I didn't suffer as badly as I might have done – so many meningitis patients lose limbs, and I didn't. I was very fortunate and I am very thankful.

I lost a huge amount of weight while I was ill in hospital. When I was admitted I weighed eighty-six kilograms and by the time I left I had dropped to seventy-two kilograms, which was closer to a good weight for me. But it wasn't long before I put it all back on. I have always battled with my weight and have yo-yoed throughout my life. Never more so than when we were expecting Junior. Katie asked me to comfort eat with her during the pregnancy, and I did. Instead of home-cooked meals we were living on takeaways and the kind of food that's not exactly good for the waistline. It was annoying because she would eat the same as me and wouldn't put an ounce of weight on. Her metabolism seemed to deal with it well and mine didn't. Part of the problem was that she would just pick at stuff, and then I would eat the rest – I don't like wasting food! I really ballooned then and I didn't lose it properly until after we split. I probably lost a bit too much to begin with, but when I'm unhappy I go off my food. You can see a dramatic difference now to some of these early pictures where I was really heavy. Some recent headlines have said I look gaunt, but I'm sensible and my weight is under control. With the rehearsals for my recent tour I managed to keep it off. I'm very focused – I've now dropped to seventy kilograms and I'm training hard. I'm not overly fussy with my diet – I combine junk and health food, eating what I want but watching the portions. Taking exercise is the key thing – that and eating good food is a million times better than starving yourself and taking no exercise. Food is one of life's greatest joys and it's wrong to deny yourself its pleasure. I love cooking and when the kids are over I will always make sure we sit down as a family and eat a home-cooked meal. I'm determined that I won't let my weight yo-yo again (well, I hope . . . LOL).

J ust a month after my meningitis scare, which was a really difficult time, we had something fantastic to celebrate: Princess Tiaamii was born on 29 June 2007. Thankfully, after the birth Katie was fine – she didn't suffer with depression the second time round, which was a big relief. You worry that that kind of thing will happen time and again, but it had been a one-off. Before Princess was born, I suggested that we name her after Amy, Katie's mum, or after my mum Tia, but again Katie wasn't keen so I came up with the idea of putting Tia and Amy together, the names of both our mums, to make Tiaamii. I would like her to be called Tiaamii all the time. It's such a pretty name and when she goes to school I think it will be better for her on a day-to-day basis than Princess. I've nicknamed her Pringles, but I am going to make a concerted effort to call her Tiaamii when she is a bit older. Like Junior, Tiaamii is very tactile and likes to cuddle. (I am determined she will become a nun – I can only imagine how overprotective I will be when she brings her first boyfriend home. What am I talking about? She will never have a boyfriend, ha ha! I can't bear to think about it. I say to her, 'Pringles, what are you going to be when you're older?' She looks at me with her big blue eyes and I'll quickly say, 'A nun, that's right, Pringles!' Thank goodness it's a few years off yet before she brings boys home. Yes, she will definitely be a nun if I have anything to do with it!) She is a beautiful child, with a beautiful nature.

'BOTH TIAAMII AND JJ HAVE A REALLY GOOD BROTHER–SISTER RELATIONSHIP AND WILL HUG EACH OTHER AND PLAY TOGETHER.'

Both Tiaamii and JJ have a really good brother–sister relationship and will hug each other and play together. If they are naughty, they will always kiss and make up – even if I have to make sure that they do! It's important that you stay close to your siblings – I have always been close with mine, so it would be lovely if they stay friends as they grow up. You rely on your brothers and sisters through good times and bad times and if JJ and Tiaamii have a good relationship it will benefit both of them. I've owned businesses with my siblings, they've played on stage with me when I've been on tour, I live with my brother Mike now and I just can't imagine not sharing my life with them. Even though some of my brothers live halfway across the world from me, we're still very close and talk all the time, and get together as a family as often as we can. That's the relationship I'd like my children to have with each other as they get older.

We went to South Africa to renew
our marriage vows in September
2008. It was an exhilarating trip

In September 2008 we went to South Africa on an amazing, magical, exhilarating holiday – it was a mind-blowing trip filled with all sorts of different activities and I loved it. We were there to renew our vows, something that Kate really wanted. If I'm honest, after just three years of marriage I thought it was too early, but she really wanted to do it and said the main reason was so that she could change her surname to Andre afterwards. That never happened. She wanted something more private than our wedding this time round and I went along with it. Although we were filming our reality TV show, Katie was adamant that she wanted the cameras to be off when we said our actual vows, which I couldn't understand. Anyway, the footage did go out on the show in the end, but you couldn't hear what we were saying to one another – music was played over it.

'I'D NEVER BEEN ON SAFARI BEFORE
AND IT WAS ONE OF THE MOST
BEAUTIFUL EXPERIENCES I HAVE EVER
HAD. I LOVED EVERY MINUTE OF IT.'

Afterwards we went on a safari. I'd never been on one before and it was one of the most beautiful experiences I have ever had. I loved every minute of it. To be at one with nature like that is extraordinary. Monkeys would sit outside our room and if we left the doors open they would come in, pinch stuff and run off. I loved it – they were so cheeky! Normally nothing would get me up at 5 a.m., other than the children, but the wildlife we were seeing was amazing and each morning I was raring to go. Overnight you could hear the animals outside – elephants, lions, the lot. You were literally living in their habitat and it's one of the most memorable trips I have been on. I seriously recommend it.

While we were over there I also went swimming with sharks – it was incredible. On the boat our cameraman Mike was puking everywhere and we'd been laughing at him but, as karma would have it, two minutes later when we hit the open waters I started to feel really seasick as well. I'm sure we were the reason that we saw so many sharks that day – we were literally feeding the fish! We were dropped down in one of those big metal-barred shark cages, and I was nervous, but weirdly not as nervous or unhappy as I would feel if I was going on a rollercoaster. Admittedly, when a great white shark came flying at the bars with its mouth wide open it was quite a shock, but I loved every minute of it. We also went whale watching and sea-lion watching. I love going out on boats on sunny days but this particular day was freezing. I can remember how cold it was even now. Every time we spotted a whale we'd run out to look and then run back inside again into the warmth. The sea lions were something else altogether – the South Africans call them Cape Fur Seals and they were lovely but, seriously, they stank! Seal is the most repugnant smell that you can imagine. (I don't know how Heidi Klum manages! Only joking, bud . . .) We also went up Table Mountain while we were there. I hate heights but for some reason I decided to go anyway. It was a sheer drop and of course I freaked out completely when I got to the top. I was crouching down to try to make things better and everyone had to coax me down because I couldn't move. I was utterly terrified up there. Put me in with the great whites any day! In fact the whole trip was one big fantastic experience – South Africa is so beautiful and reminds me a lot of Australia.

My life has been full of interesting experiences, and another one of these was my duet with Katie singing 'A Whole New World'. We originally did it for Children in Need in 2005, but it was received so well that we were asked to release it as a single. First of all the charity had asked us to perform some ballroom dancing but we thought that was tacky. But singing 'A Whole New World' from the Disney cartoon *Aladdin* wasn't, right? Anyway, we chose to do the duet and our performance got a huge response. Claire and Neville went to see some of the record labels that wanted to release it and agreed that they could have an album of duets from Katie and me if they also offered us solo deals. I was used to how cutthroat the industry was and how much effort you have to put in to make it work, but the proceeds of the album were split between five different charities. Katie had singing lessons – I'd been having mine for years but Katie had just started – we had to take it seriously if we wanted it to be a success. We finally released the album *A Whole New World* in 2006. It didn't exactly add to my musical credibility but people liked it! We shot the video in Rome – a beautiful place. I wanted to sightsee while I was there because my passion for everything Italian is so great but unfortunately there was no time. We just shot the video and came home again. I enjoyed that trip, but I would have loved to have stayed longer and soaked up a bit more of Italy. (Sometimes I think I must be Italian rather than Greek. Food is really important to me and, although I like Greek food, pasta is my favourite! I said to my dad the other day, 'Dad, are you sure I'm Greek? I feel more Italian. I love the people, I love the culture and I love the food.' Just kidding, I love my Greek heritage with all my heart . . . but I could be Italian!)

Another place I've been that I loved was Dubai. When I was younger I went out for a *Hello!* magazine photoshoot and I loved it. It wasn't so built up then and it was great being there. I love the culture of Dubai, and the people. The food is great and it feels as though it's the whole world in one city. A bit of New York, a bit of London, a bit of Rome, a bit of everything really. I went there again when I was with Katie to film for our TV show, but she wasn't as keen on the place as me. I'm hoping to go out again this year and take the kids – perhaps we'll get in some sand-surfing this time as well as relaxing!

'I'M HOPING TO GO OUT AGAIN THIS YEAR AND TAKE THE KIDS – PERHAPS WE'LL GET IN SOME SAND-SURFING THIS TIME AS WELL AS RELAXING!'

My life was pretty well documented by that point – we had video cameras following us more or less everywhere, filming our reality TV series. At first, it felt very strange but you learn to ignore them and after a while there are times when you forget they are there at all. I'm still filming my reality show, *The Next Chapter*, but at the moment I'm glad it's just in the UK. There are talks of trying to launch my reality show in Australia and possibly doing a tour, but I've said that, as much as I'd love to do that, there's something that really scares me about it because at the moment Australia is a place I can escape to, a get-out for me. I haven't done anything out there for a while and although I was massive there back in the 1990s I am more well known in the UK now. For me, that's a nice balance, because when I go over to Oz I can have some quiet time, some me time. If the programme was shown out there, that might not be the case. It's pretty full-on over here. If you go out of your house at any time of the day or night someone will be waiting to see you, picture you or speak to you. I'm not knocking it one bit, I don't begrudge it because I love the Great British Public, they've been amazing; but it's nice to be anonymous at times and in Australia I can be. If I didn't have children I would have gone back a year ago. I love England, but I needed my family when Katie and I split and they were out there.

Going forward, I keep thinking that the next girl I date will be someone out of the spotlight, a non-celebrity who will also prefer a quieter life. But how do you know who you will fall in love with? I hope when it happens I'll know. I'd like it to blast me over – to see someone and to just know. I am longing for that feeling.

THE END SPELLS A NEW BEGINNING

I N FEBRUARY 2009, WE WENT AS A FAMILY TO THE USA, TO LIVE IN LOS ANGELES FOR THREE MONTHS. WE WEREN'T GOING OUT TO TRY TO BREAK AMERICA, BUT IT WAS AN OPPORTUNITY FOR BOTH OF US TO TRY SOMETHING NEW. I WANTED TO START WRITING MUSIC AGAIN AND PRODUCING MY OWN WORK, AND WE DECIDED TO GO OUT THERE AND FILM OUR SHOW, *KATIE AND PETER: STATESIDE*.

The trip was always going to be fairly full-on but I thought it would be a good opportunity to spend some time away from the mayhem of the UK and do something different as a family. Despite the reports, there were never any plans to move away from the UK and stay in the US long-term, this was simply a combined holiday and business trip. I've always said I'd like to live in LA because it is so much closer to Australia, that much nearer to my family, but it was never an option and I knew that. Kate would never have wanted to leave her family in the UK behind (even while we were out there her sister Sophie and mum Amy were with us a lot) and I understood that. I know how hard it is to be away from your loved ones and I would never have asked her to make that sort of sacrifice. On the flip side, in my opinion there were a lot of benefits to us being in Los Angeles. Neither of us were recognized as much in LA, which for me was a good thing. There were loads of paparazzi that followed us around who'd sell the pictures back to the UK, but mostly the Americans had and still don't have an idea of who we are, so although we were followed more than the UK it was solely to sell the pictures back to the UK. Most importantly, being in the States did Harvey a world of good. For that reason alone I would have stayed there longer. He came on leaps and bounds at the school he attended. It was incredible: we have a lot to thank that school for, they did wonders for his progression.

THE HOUSE IN LA WHERE WE STAYED
FOR THREE MONTHS WAS MASSIVE.
THE KIDS ABSOLUTELY LOVED IT

We rented a beautiful house in Malibu (in the same area that Britney Spears and Jennifer Aniston lived, apparently, so we were in good company!) Anyone who watched the show saw that it had everything you could ever want or need. The house was massive: seven bedrooms and seven bathrooms, plus a huge swimming pool, a tennis court, a pond and nature trails in the grounds and stables. The views were amazing, you could see the mountains and the ocean. It was absolutely incredible and the kids loved it. The weather was perfect and I could do what I love to do best . . . barbecue! If I had had my way I would have cooked that way every night, I love it so much. The barbecue area was right by the pool and it felt very romantic out there in the evenings: barbecue going, candles lit, warm air – it really was idyllic. To top it all off, and the cherry on the cake for me, was that I was there to write music, my passion. All the things I loved were in one place – *perfetto*, or so I thought.

I had always wanted an opportunity to have creative input into my music, rather than being guided by a record company or a producer. So I invested a lot of money, £200,000 to be precise, and a huge amount of time, trying to realize that dream and create a new album that I could finally be proud of. When I started on this project I had no idea where it was going – all I knew was that I wanted to produce a new album that gave me credibility and that was different to anything I'd done before. It seemed the perfect opportunity to do it; we were going to LA to film and spend some time with the kids in the Sunshine State and it seemed like the time was right to put my money where my mouth was. By 2009 it had been five years since my last album, *The Long Road Back*. Releasing new music after such a long time, especially music that is so different to what you've done before, is risky, nerve-racking. It was very daunting: I had a lot riding on it and was desperate to make it work. While I was out there I got to collaborate with some great names and loved every minute. AC Burrell, who used to be in So Solid Crew, was brilliant to work with, as was Kevin McPherson and the amazing Francesca Richard. Francesca helped me to put my lyrics together. She assisted me so much with the new way of writing I was developing. I would tell her what and how I was feeling, exactly what I wanted to sing about, she would make sense of it all and then we would put the lyrics together. She hit the nail on the head every time and in each song we managed to sum up very succinctly just how I was feeling at the time. She was brilliant and I can't thank her enough for her help. In fact, AC, too, really helped me see a vision for this album, as did the person who introduced me to him, Richard Pascoe. Our relative anonymity in the US made it easy for me to get around and after spending time with the family in the day I'd go to the studio in the evening and hibernate for hours on end. Making music has always meant so much to me and this was such a fantastic opportunity that I wanted to take advantage of every spare minute in the studio with these guys helping me. I'd lose hours in there, the time

While I was happy, Katie wasn't. For us it was like a role reversal. She was the one who was used to working all the time, in the UK there was always something she was out and about doing – photoshoots or promoting a range or a new book. But in America it was different. She was mainly there for the TV show, and because I had the dream of recording again I knew I would be away from the family for too long if they didn't all come with me. We did do some photoshoots for magazines over there, as well as some TV and radio, and our management secured a chat show of our own too. But mostly I was the one working while she stayed at home or went shopping. Until this point it was me who was used to being in the shadow – yes, I never stopped writing music but I wasn't recording, or in the limelight in the same way as Katie. Now for the first time the boot was on the other foot. Katie found it really hard to adapt. I wanted so much for her to be a part of it all. So many times I would ask her to come to the studio with me but she wouldn't, she just didn't seem interested in what I was doing. Saying that, when I played her the first recording of 'Call the Doctor' and the later recording of 'Unconditional' she absolutely loved them. Other than that she didn't show much interest. I'm not saying anything here that you couldn't watch back: I'm sure that if you look at the episode of *Stateside* where she did come down to the studio, her reaction said it all. She just didn't want to know, or that's how it felt. It seemed there was nothing I could do to change her mind or make things better. The cracks were really beginning to show to the outside world: the press were picking up on our rows in the show which had moved up a gear, and there seemed to be leaks everywhere, journalists being told that behind closed doors we were fighting more than ever – it wasn't nice for either of us.

'IN THAT HEAT I CAN TELL YOU IT WASN'T EASY TO TRAIN, BUT IT WAS SOMETHING WE BOTH REALLY WANTED TO DO. PLENTY OF PICTURES OF ME AND KATIE TRYING TO GET FIT WERE TAKEN AND PRINTED.'

As well as working on the album and putting in the hours for our television show, Katie and I also started to train for the London marathon in April, three months away. Having let my weight creep up again, I wanted to use the time in LA to shift a few pounds and get fit. I think your body changes when you get into your thirties and you have to work a bit harder to stay trim – I know I do, even now the weight is off I have to work hard at the look. I like to get fit the old-fashioned way – Rocky-style training is the way to go! In that heat I can tell you it wasn't easy to train, but it was something we both really wanted to do. Plenty of pictures of me and Katie trying to get fit were taken and printed – people seemed to like watching us sweat while running along the sea front! The marathon was a real challenge but one I have always wanted to try and conquer. When we started I couldn't imagine being able to run that far and getting to the end in one piece, but we did it. We hired a personal trainer and we did it the correct way, building ourselves up gradually and working our way closer and closer to the twenty-six miles that we needed to be fit enough to run in April 2009.

I was trying really hard to eat healthily. In LA there is a real pressure to look your best all the time – it's a place where the 'perfect' people live, and it's very easy to get sucked into that way of thinking very quickly. It's not difficult to check yourself into a clinic and come out a few days later with a whole new look. Whiter than white teeth, bigger breasts, a waist to die for . . . you get the picture! If you like that sort of thing then it's okay, but almost everyone has that look and when you walk down the street people seem to morph into one another after a while. For me a bit of identity and individuality is nice!

So the Los Angeles trip was a busy time, I was living on adrenalin and loving writing my music. But it signalled the lowest point for my relationship with Katie, and I don't think it was a huge surprise to anyone when we finally announced our separation on that fateful day, 11 May 2009.

THEY THINK IT'S ALL OVER... IT IS NOW

O N THE DAY OF THE SPLIT OUR MANAGEMENT SENT OUT A STATEMENT: 'PETER ANDRE AND KATIE PRICE ARE SEPARATING AFTER FOUR-AND-A-HALF YEARS.' IT WAS OVER. FINITO. DONE. SADLY, AS SOME CYNICS HAD PREDICTED, THE MARRIAGE HAD COLLAPSED.

Walking away is a strength, not a weakness – anyone who thinks otherwise is mistaken. Believe me, it was not an easy decision for me to walk out on my marriage, and not one that was taken lightly. But it had to be done – there was no other option. People who ask the question, 'Why is he upset? He left his family', just to make it clear I left Katie, not my children, but if people knew why I left her they would more than understand my hurt. The consequences of my decision hit me properly about five weeks after I'd left. I went shopping in Ikea because I needed to buy some things for the new place and the reality of what was happening felt like a slap around the face. I had to start all over again. Mike and Claire were trying to keep me positive but the realization that this was final was beginning to hit home. I was looking at new furniture and new belongings for my new house. There was no 'our' any more. There wasn't anyone else's opinion I had to take into consideration – it was suddenly all down to me. Simply put, my heart just wasn't in it. I knew I needed to get the necessary furniture, but as I was looking through it all my head was somewhere else altogether. My belongings were still at the marital home – in fact they still are – but I haven't been back to get them. As time goes on I know I need to sort it all out, it's just that it hasn't been a priority for me.

OUR LAST CHRISTMAS TOGETHER AS A FAMILY IN 2008

I didn't expect our marriage to end in divorce and definitely not as soon as it did. When I look back at our last Christmas together as a family in 2008 and the pictures of us all unwrapping presents I could never have imagined that it was going to be the last one together. Ever since I've had children Christmas has become a big deal – the day is all about the kids and they come first; it's their day, and that Christmas was no exception. We had a fantastic day filled with huge amounts of excitement, presents and great food. The house was decorated from top to toe in Christmas decorations with a Christmas tree either side of the staircase – it was like Santa's grotto! Father Christmas had visited by the time the kids woke up, which surprisingly wasn't too early. They were all so excited and had been for days. First one up was Tiaamii, then Junior and finally Harvey. Tiaamii didn't come into our room until about 8 a.m., which is pretty good! But once they were up the excitement on their faces was adorable and they couldn't wait to get stuck into their presents.

The children were spoiled as usual: they had so many presents and it was a joy to see them ripping off the wrapping paper, they were so excited. Harvey doesn't like the sound of paper ripping, but once he'd got to the presents he too loved every minute of it! I know the kids are spoiled on Christmases and birthdays, but without sounding like a bore, I am very keen that they are brought up with an idea of the value of money, just like I was. I don't want them to have everything they want on demand just because we're able to do that for them, although I do spoil them, I can't lie! They don't get everything they want all year round and I think that's very important. Whether or not they are already sorted financially, I would like them to pursue careers of their own. They will all have their own dreams and aspirations, and I'd like to see those realized.

Once the presents were unwrapped and the kids were happily playing with everything we all mucked in getting lunch ready – a proper Christmas dinner, with all the trimmings. There were loads of us, so we all helped with the preparations. All of Katie's family came over, as well as my brother Mike, so we had a full house. Originally I had suggested that we go to Australia for Christmas to see my family but Katie wanted to spend it with her folks and I understood that. I knew she wanted to be around her family and that that was important to her so I let it go, but in my heart of hearts I thought it would have been a great opportunity to visit my parents and for the kids to see their grandparents and cousins. We saw my parents so infrequently that any time off that we had I wanted to try to get out to Australia and see them as a family, but it wasn't to be. We had a wonderful day that year, though: I dressed up as Father Christmas and really got into the spirit, and the kids loved it.

Last Christmas was my first as a father on my own. I had the kids until 6 p.m. on Christmas Day, so I was determined to make the most of every minute. On Christmas Eve, we put out milk and cookies for Father Christmas, and carrots for the reindeer. We had never done that before and the kids were so excited. I made sure that I wrapped all the presents in secret and hid them away in the garage so the kids couldn't find them. I even put batteries in everything that needed them, so that the kids could play with their new toys. It was weird and different because it wasn't what we were used to, but it was lovely all the same, and I wanted to keep things traditional in every way. I wanted as little disruption as possible – I planned the whole thing meticulously – and as far as the children were concerned they got to have two Christmases. It has been strange doing things solo for the first time – even Junior and Tiaamii's birthdays have been very different. The kids love it, of course, it means they get two lots of presents but for me it was a real learning curve. Organizing the food and the cake and the friends. We had great fun, it was just different. But it's a different I am learning to get used to and adapt to.

2009 WAS MY FIRST CHRISTMAS AS
A SINGLE PARENT. I SPENT IT WITH
MIKE, PRINCESS AND JUNIOR

'ON CHRISTMAS EVE, WE PUT OUT MILK AND COOKIES FOR FATHER CHRISTMAS, AND CARROTS FOR THE REINDEER. WE HAD NEVER DONE THAT BEFORE AND THE KIDS WERE SO EXCITED. I MADE SURE THAT I WRAPPED ALL THE PRESENTS IN SECRET AND HID THEM AWAY IN THE GARAGE SO THE KIDS COULDN'T FIND THEM.'

JUNIOR AND TIAAMII'S BIRTHDAYS
HAVE BEEN VERY DIFFERENT
SINCE THE SPLIT, WITH BOTH
KATE AND I THROWING PARTIES
FOR THEM. THE KIDS LOVE IT
OF COURSE, IT MEANS THEY GET
TWO LOTS OF PRESENTS. BUT
FOR ME IT HAS BEEN A REAL
LEARNING CURVE

'THE DAY I GAVE UP ON THE MARRIAGE ONCE AND FOR ALL WAS THE DAY I LEFT. BEFORE THAT I HAD EVERY INTENTION OF STANDING BY AND MAKING THINGS WORK, AND THAT'S THE TRUTH.'

The day I gave up on the marriage once and for all was the day I left. Before that I had every intention of standing by and making things work, and that's the truth. But once I walked out of that door, having made the hardest decision of my life, I knew it was over forever. I knew that there was no going back. I was vulnerable at first and if there were any doubts in my head, it was because of the children. But I was resolute. Because my mum and dad have been married for such a long time I felt such a failure with my marriage breaking down. I had become one of the statistics and sadly the ideal of marriage for life that I once so believed in wasn't meant to be in this case. When I took my vows I meant them, sincerely I meant every word. For me, it was for life – not a bit of fun. Needless to say, having to phone Mum and Dad to tell them was one of the hardest hurdles to get over. On the phone they could hear my pain and devastation. I was in a real state. They were both so understanding and supportive about the situation; there was no judgement from them or difficult questions asked. They understood that I had my reasons and they knew, as only parents can, how I was feeling. They knew that I would have done everything in my power to make it work, they didn't even need to ask.

My parents have always supported me whatever I chose to do but it hasn't always been easy for them to agree with some of my choices because I haven't led what most people would call a 'normal' life. Instead, from an early age, I've led a life that's been in the public eye. In an ideal world my parents would have liked me to have stayed well away from this industry in the first place. It always worried my dad in particular. His main concern was that the industry was quite corrupt and that I would get led astray. Mum and Dad associated the music business with sex, drugs and rock 'n' roll. (Two out of the three I have fallen prey to, I'll admit, but drugs have never been on my agenda. I feel very strongly about that. It's an easy trap to fall in to because they are commonplace in many circles, but I was never tempted – they are a big no-no in my book.) In many ways I think my parents were right to be worried, it is a pretty messed-up industry and when you first start out you're naïve, you don't realize that. It's imperative to have strong people around you, making sure that you stay sensible – it's very easy to get led astray.

MIKE AND I LIVE TOGETHER
IN BRIGHTON. HE HAS BEEN
AN EXTREMELY SUPPORTIVE
BROTHER AND IS AN
AMAZING UNCLE

Once they saw that I was going to stay grounded (aside from a few blips along the way!) Mum and Dad had a bit more trust and faith in me and accepted my choices. Of course they had reservations about me getting married so quickly but I'm sure that would have been the case whoever I had chosen. They wanted to be sure that it was the right thing for their son and such a speedy engagement had alarm bells ringing in their heads. They wanted assurances that we both knew what we were doing, that we had got to know each other fully before making such a massive commitment. I thought we had. Never in my wildest dreams did I imagine that things would go so terribly wrong and that the hurt caused to everyone involved could be so great. Perhaps if I'd known then I would never have done it, but as I say, love is blind and it wouldn't have mattered what anyone said to me at the time, I was going to marry her no matter what the consequences.

This massive life-changing experience for me was lived out by everyone around me too – they had seen all my emotions over the years, the ups, the downs and now finally the tears. All of my family rallied round to help, they could see how low I was and I think deep down they were really worried that I'd end up relapsing into depression like before. Mike has been with me ever since the split and has been fantastic. He now lives with me in Brighton but my sister Debbie was also particularly protective of me. It was nice to get the female perspective from her and to have someone who I could talk things through with. She helped me a lot in the early days, right after I walked out, and could empathize with the emotions I was experiencing. Brothers are great, but they have a much more 'pull yourself together' attitude and I needed to wallow for a bit. I needed to pour my heart out and she was there to listen and advise. The whole family was very supportive, and if we could get any closer than we already were, then we did. It's a very Mediterranean thing to be so protective, so close, despite being halfway across the world from one another. It's like blood is everything. We are very passionate about our families and would die for our own, that's the truth – that's the way we were brought up.

Central Park, New York - Classic Photography by Ralf Uicker

Unfortunately, I have had one panic attack after the split. It was after I saw pictures of the kids playing with a boyfriend of Kate's. I found it unbelievably hard to see Junior and Princess with another man around them so soon. I think that is any father's nightmare, and I went to bed that night feeling upset and anxious. I'm pretty sure that's what brought on the attack. I woke up and knew something was wrong, I didn't feel well at all, so I went to ask Mike to take me to the hospital. But I must have collapsed on the way to getting him. When I woke up there was blood all over me. I'd blacked out, and whacked my head. I couldn't move for about half an hour I was so dazed and confused, but it was a real wake-up call – it was important that I looked after myself and surrounded myself by people that cared and watched out for me.

Following the split it was just a matter of weeks before I had to start promoting the new album I'd worked on in the US, which I'd named *Revelation*. Journalists being journalists (it's their job, I know!) wanted to ask me the tricky stuff, the stuff I'd rather not go into. Far more interesting to them than my music was my failed marriage and inevitably that was what I was quizzed on. I'm not griping, I get it, but it wasn't particularly easy for me. As I've reiterated, I didn't (and still don't) want to go into detail, and also I was grieving. I think I've proven quite publicly that I'm an emotional guy, and because things were still so raw at that stage any personal questions got to me easily. I didn't want to break down and for everyone to see me crying – although that has now happened. The first television interview I did was for *This Morning* – it was one of Fern Britton's last days and I felt privileged to have been asked on the show. Inevitably, questions were asked about my personal life and I was visibly shaking; you could see my hands jumping up and down. I think that a lot of people were surprised to see how much weight I'd lost at that point. I looked really quite skinny in comparison to how they knew me, how I'd looked just a few weeks before. But I can't eat when I'm under such stress, so the weight had dropped off me. The weight loss, coupled with my hands shaking and my inability to talk about the subject meant that people were a bit worried about me, I think. But everyone deals with situations differently

and you don't know until something like that happens how you will be, how it will affect you physically and emotionally. I remember trying to explain why I didn't want to talk about it which I knew was frustrating for them but I couldn't handle it at the time. I remember saying something like, 'Would you forgive me if I don't answer that question? Would that be rude?' I was trying to be so polite and yet inside I was dying. I think viewers could see how uncomfortable I was and I hope they knew that I really wasn't trying to be difficult! Fern and Phil were simply doing their job and asking me what, understandably, everyone wanted to know. I worry about these things coming over wrong, or that people will think badly of me – I'm a great worrier. But I'm sure ITV were okay about it because I'm now working on *This Morning* and loving every minute!

Immediately after leaving Kate, I moved into Claire and Neville's house temporarily until I sorted out more permanent accommodation. Mike gave up his place in east London to come and be with me as well, and had to commute to London every day for work. It was just what I needed at the time, to be around people who cared and who understood. Claire never told me what to do, just listened and looked after me. Her son, Nysna, helped take my mind off things too – being separated from my children for the first time was tough and being around another child really helped me. The house was big and there was lots to do so when the kids came for the first couple of visits we didn't need to go out, and stayed in feeding the ducks, chickens and geese. We'd all watch movies together or go swimming – I felt safe from everything there. But after the initial onslaught of stories in the press I decided that I needed to get out of the country. I needed space to be on my own, without reading the inevitable, and ongoing, headlines. I couldn't face them. I escaped to Cyprus, my bolt-hole.

'IT WAS AMAZING TO BE ABLE TO BUILD SOMETHING FROM SCRATCH AND BECAUSE OF THAT INPUT, IT'S SO PERSONAL TO ME AND MY FAMILY. IT'S VERY INDULGENT, BUT IT'S MY PLACE TO ESCAPE TO AND I LOVE BEING THERE.'

Before I went into *I'm A Celebrity . . .* I bought some land in Cyprus with the idea of building my perfect house on it, and I've done just that. I bought the land about ten years ago and I love being there – I'd go there tomorrow if I could. Mum and Dad gave up their life so that the house in Cyprus could be built. They left their beautiful home in Australia and moved to a two-bedroom flat in Larnaca so that they could oversee the build. It was Dad's dream to build a house from scratch in Cyprus, and between us we came up with the designs for the house. Although I couldn't be there to oversee it, Dad wanted to work with the architects to make sure everything was in order and correct, so for three years my parents lived there and made sure that the dream house was built. I owe them so much for that – their home in Australia is fantastic and yet they were prepared to leave it behind and move into a small apartment for three years of their lives. The outcome of all the hard work and time that my parents gave up is this incredible house that I'd one day like to call home. The climate is great all year round, it's private and it's beautiful. It was amazing to be able to build something from scratch and because of that input, it's so personal to me and my family. It's very indulgent, but it's my place to escape to and I love being there. Outside, there are huge heart-shaped stones with lights which are a real statement and look incredible when lit up at night. The kitchen is beautiful, it's blood red and I had it shipped over from England. Chris Jay, who owns the kitchen company that fitted it for me, was amazing and as long as he's in business I will always get him to fit my kitchens! He really went that extra mile to get it just how I wanted. My uncle looks after the house while I'm away and goes to check on it every day, which gives me peace of mind while I'm not there. It's a happy place – it makes me smile just thinking about it – and I wish I could go there more. I love taking the kids out there; it is a part of me and a part of their history.

ONE OF THE SHOTS THE PAPARAZZI TOOK OF ME BREAKING DOWN AS I HUGGED MY MOTHER

On this occasion the children came with me, which was lovely, and Mike and our cuz Angelo were also with us – I needed my family around me and the kids really made sure that I couldn't dwell on things too much. I didn't want them to see me upset so it kept me strong. When I'm in Cyprus I feel away from everything, cut off from the real world, and it gave me time to try and get my head together before facing the music when I got back. The press had taken snaps of me leaving the country but I was putting a brave face on things and I wasn't about to break down for them to see. But when my mum flew in to be with us I cracked, and the paparazzi captured it all. Those pictures were splashed all across the newspapers and magazines and I could see from looking at them the state I'd got myself into. Cynics said that I was putting it on for the cameras. Really, I can't believe people could say that I was capable of doing that. Anyone who knows me knows that I was a broken man. My heart was in pieces and seeing my mum allowed me to drop my guard. At times like that you need your parents, only they can help make things better. That was the first time I'd properly broken down since I'd walked away. Until then, I think my body had run out of tears, in a way. I had done my crying during the marriage, when things were at rock bottom.

To see my Mum in Cyprus after everything I'd been through was incredibly emotional. In times of need like that, your parents are the best medicine. Although everything we'd been through was still there, hanging over us like a dark cloud, we actually had a lovely holiday. Mum is a fantastic grandmother: my only wish is that she and Dad could see their grandchildren more. Mum would love to be around her grandchildren every day which sadly isn't possible, so when she is with them she makes the most of every second.

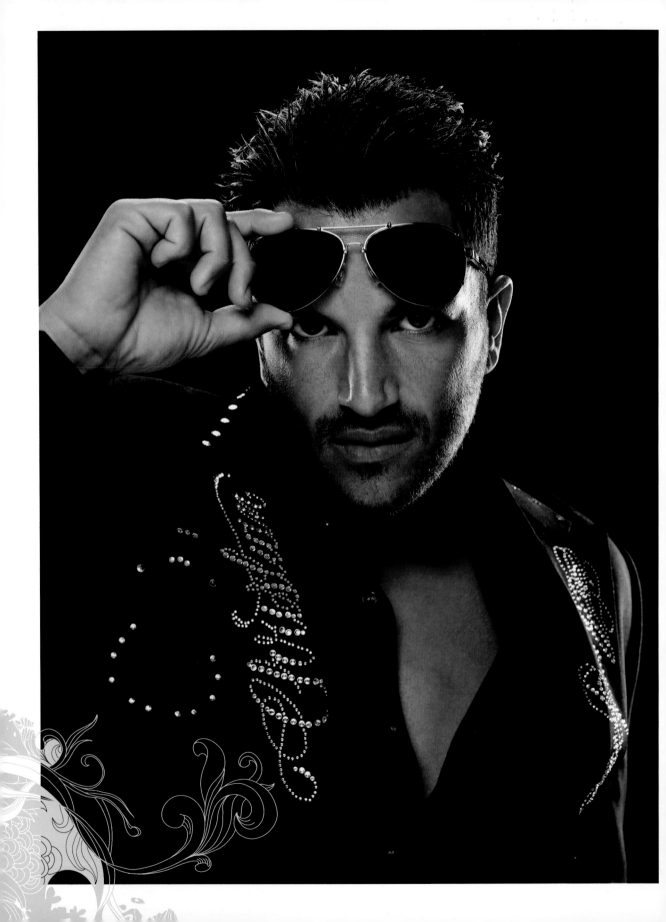

ONWARDS AND UPWARDS

THE OLD SAYING THAT TIME IS A GREAT HEALER IS TRUE. I'M GETTING MYSELF BACK TOGETHER. I'M ALMOST THERE, I'M SURE. SOME DAYS THERE ARE SETBACKS BUT I AM ONLY HUMAN AND THAT'S TO BE EXPECTED. A lot of people go through separation and it is so hard when you have children and all the kids want is for their mum and dad to be together. It's been incredibly difficult, and it's also been hard for me not to speak out and set the record straight at times.

Whatever has gone on between Katie and I should wherever possible not involve our children directly. Bad-mouthing each other will only hurt them. I'm not looking forward to having to answer the children's questions when they finally see, read and understand what's gone on. Headlines are dismissible – you can find an answer, an excuse and explain them away – but you can't dismiss the pictures. I will do everything in my power to protect my kids when that time comes. These days, any hurt that I feel is for them, when I know they are being affected. I can't lie and say it's easy to see my kids with another man but it was always going to happen and all I can really ask for is a man who remains a constant for them. I don't want them seeing different men coming in and out – children don't understand that and get hurt every time a relationship ends. If he's a good guy and kind with the kids then that is the best I can ask for. When I'm dating I want to make sure any relationship is the real deal before I officially introduce a girlfriend to the children. I said I would remain celibate until after my divorce and I have always been true to my word. What I do now is up to me, but I will not flaunt anything in front of the children. There definitely won't be any kind of intimacy in front of the kids and I mean of any kind, not until she officially becomes my girlfriend – I can promise that. I feel really strongly about this.

Nowadays, I am concentrating on the time I get with the children and my music career, which has really taken off. I'm not deluded, I know that I still have a lot to prove musically and a long way to go, but I'm producing songs that mean something to me and that people actually seem to like. Phew! Even with the recent success that I've had, most radio stations still won't play my music, but instead of being bitter about it, like I might have been before, I understand. I accept it. I've learned that it's important for me to turn the negatives into positives and keep going. With time, I hope that I might get those stations to play my music. Eventually I think it can happen. All I have to do is keep working on improving. You've got to be persistent and that's exactly what I am – my chequered career has shown that! The music I worked on in America was different to anything I'd ever turned out, but no record label would touch it, they still weren't willing to give me a chance. I know the record companies thought it wouldn't work, that I was wasting my time, but I was determined to prove them wrong. So against all the odds I ploughed my money in and locked myself in the studio to try to make the best album possible. Truthfully, I had no idea how well it would do, it was a massive gamble. Fortunately it was a gamble that paid off – one year on and the album has gone platinum. I want to sing that from the rooftops it makes me so proud! By taking the risk and going it alone, I always had the final say. It was a vanity project and I was paying the bill. This was personal and I was determined to make it a success. I didn't have a big record label breathing down my neck or taking decisions out of my hands, I got to do it my way for once. I got to work on something that I truly believed in and ultimately a product that was commercial too. I think people were genuinely surprised how different it was. In some ways the pressure is greater when you are doing it all by yourself because you want to make the best music possible. That was certainly the case with me. Now it's done so well there are a lot of opportunities being thrown my way. So you see, the moral of the story is, don't give up on your dreams. You have got to keep going. *Revelation* went platinum with the backing of an independent record label, Conehead, who shared my vision at the last minute and I'm very grateful to them. But it was proof that even with minimal airtime on the radio it's possible to succeed.

Revelation is my favourite album to date because I got to have so much say over it, although *Time*, back in the late 1990s, I'm also very proud of because I got to work alongside some amazing artists like Brian McKnight, Coolio, Montell Jordan and Diane Warren. Revelation was riskier than any of my previous albums because it was so different and people might not have liked my new direction. I'd gone from writing songs based on melodies to songs based on lyrics, songs written from the heart, and I just had to hope people liked it.

After I'd finished writing the tracks in LA, I needed to choose which ones would make the final cut and end up as part of *Revelation*. In America, when you have finished writing an album you invite people – producers, backing singers, friends, family, basically anyone you want an opinion from – to come and listen to the songs: it's called a Listening Party. I had written seventeen tracks and had to choose just eleven so it was important that I got people's opinions and a listening party was the perfect opportunity to get an insight into what people really thought. Ultimately everyone there felt more or less the same about the tracks and in the end it wasn't difficult to decide which ones would make the final cut.

The launch party at Studio Valbonne in the West End of London was a big deal for me: I could showcase a few of the songs and gauge a reaction. It was an acoustic set, which is the way I prefer to sing, and that gave me an opportunity to showcase my vocals. Often your voice can get lost in the backing music. I sang 'Behind Closed Doors', 'Call the Doctor', 'Go Back' and 'Unconditional'. It was an emotional night, but I managed to hold it together until the very end of the evening when I finally snapped and got emotional to say the least.

'**B**ehind Closed Doors' was the first song I released from the album and although many people think I wrote it after the split, I didn't. I wrote it several months before I left. It was never meant to be a statement to the public; at the time it was like therapy for me to write down exactly how I was feeling. I have already talked about our time in LA: it wasn't the happiest part of our married life, by far, and many of the songs on *Revelation* highlight that. Also, when we had counselling a year before we officially split I decided to put my feelings into songs which at the time Katie loved. Some of the songs on the album have serious lyrics and they were written eight months before I left, so even then you can see how I was feeling about things. Of course people have read into every word and have applied them to my relationship with Katie. It was all straight from the heart and people know that what I'm singing means a lot to me and, in a way, does tell a story. 'Behind Closed Doors' is pretty self-explanatory really and was heavily analysed by the press when it was released, but other songs on the album are also heartfelt and give an insight into how I was feeling when I was writing them. The words to 'Distance', (track two on the album) 'Call the Doctor', (track five) and 'Go Back', (track six) are all pretty heavy when you look at the lyrics. In the second verse of 'Distance' I sing:

> 'The honeymoon was perfect
>
> Every day was worth it
>
> The reason I said, "Yeah, I do."
>
> But as the time went on it started to unfold
>
> You're not the person that I once knew.
>
> . . . it's getting kind of complicated
>
> I don't think you understand the rules
>
> Maybe we should separate it
>
> And find the truth.'

The chorus says:

> 'I've gotta go now
>
> Gotta pack my bags and leave you alone now
>
> No more turning back
>
> . . . So we can look at it.'

THE VIDEO FOR 'BEHIND CLOSED DOORS'

'Distance' was written at a time when I thought there was hope for us and that perhaps we just needed some space – space to miss one another and learn to appreciate one another again. You can see how long ago I wrote these tracks and how I hadn't given up: I still had hope, so when it was suggested that I conveniently used the situation to promote my music it's clearly not true. The album was always going to come out in the summer, and besides, I would never do that. 'Call the Doctor' was a song that Kate loved while we were together, even though ironically those lyrics couldn't have been more real than they are now. People can take from those lyrics what they will. It says:

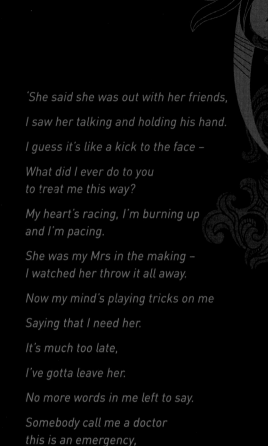

'She said she was out with her friends,

I saw her talking and holding his hand.

I guess it's like a kick to the face –

What did I ever do to you
to treat me this way?

My heart's racing, I'm burning up
and I'm pacing.

She was my Mrs in the making –
I watched her throw it all away.

Now my mind's playing tricks on me

Saying that I need her.

It's much too late,

I've gotta leave her.

No more words in me left to say.

Somebody call me a doctor
this is an emergency,

My lady's stepping out on me.

My heart's stopped beating and
now it's getting hard to breathe

Somebody call me a doctor.'

'Go Back' also has poignant lyrics. I was trying to explain that I would do anything to make things go back to the way they once were. It used to be so good, why couldn't it be like that again? I sing:

'I just wanna start back loving you the way I did before.

Tell me can we go back – if this love is real, what we waiting for?

Okay let me get this straight, you say we never communicate.

We're always at each other; we forgot how to love each other.''

The song 'Unconditional' means the most to me now. It was written about Harvey and the unconditional love I feel for him. Harvey taught me to be a father before I became a biological dad myself and I don't think anyone had written a song about that relationship before. Neville suggested I pen a song about Harvey three years ago. I was always talking about him and he said, 'Why don't you write a song about it?' And I couldn't . . . I couldn't express my feelings properly. I couldn't put it in the right words. I knew what I wanted to say but I just couldn't get it right and for Harvey it had to be perfect. And then all of a sudden it just happened, it all clicked into place. Harvey responds really well to music and now I'm not with him every day when I speak to him I will sing down the phone, and he loves it. I hope that one day he will know that this song is for him, and that he means the world to me. The fact that he's not mine by blood makes no difference to me. 'Unconditional' was not only the most expensive song on the album, with a live choir and live string section, but we got to record it where Michael Jackson recorded with his gospel choir, so for me that was the ultimate, and the absolute best for Harvey. But singing 'Unconditional' at the launch was very difficult.

STILLS FROM THE 'UNCONDITIONAL' VIDEO

LEFT: ME WITH NICOLA PARTRIDGE, AT THE *REVELATION* LAUNCH PARTY

BELOW: FROM LEFT TO RIGHT, MIKE, ME, DEBBIE AND DANNY

RIGHT: HAVING FUN WITH NEVILLE AND CLAIRE

The night of the launch was one of mixed emotions throughout not only because I wanted it to go well, for people to like what they were hearing, but also because I was singing about situations that were still raw and things that meant a lot to me. By the time I got to 'Unconditional', all eyes were on me and I was singing about someone that I love but can't be with all the time. I could feel my voice breaking, but somehow I managed to get through it. It was still such a relatively new situation for me, to be away from my family and not to see them every day, and my nerves could still be easily hit. With so many emotions flying around it was a wonder that I kept it together until afterwards. The television crew following me for my ITV2 show *Going It Alone* captured exactly how upset I got. I went offstage and everything came pouring out. I lost it, a bit like I did in Cyprus just after the split when I saw my mum. This time, it was like months of upset finally worked its way to the surface.

Backstage at the launch I was crying and hugging Neville and Claire, who was also in tears – they had lived through the pain with me and they were so proud that I'd made it this far and that I'd got through the set without cracking. Something that has really upset me throughout this difficult period is when my management, particularly my manager Claire, are continually blamed.

They have stood by me and that's it. They haven't influenced me and they certainly didn't tell me to leave Katie, and have never once said I can't be friends with her – that's complete rubbish. (I do have my own mind despite what some people might think! My management has supported me through some of the lowest times I have ever been through. They only want the best for me and the kids, so to accuse them of anything is really unfair and makes me very angry. Claire wanted to stay friends with Kate, but it wasn't to be. So let's leave the blame and slandering to one side.) To say thank you to Claire, over Christmas I bought her a car she really wanted – a yellow Beetle! I didn't tell her, it was a complete surprise. I ordered it and then got them to deliver it to her house. She was watching TV when the doorbell rang. She opened the door to be greeted by this guy who said, 'I've got a delivery for you, Ms Powell – a new car.' Because she knew nothing about it she was completely confused and tried to send him away: 'No, I haven't ordered a new car – you have the wrong person, I'm afraid.' They were in on the surprise, so they said, 'No, no, we definitely have the right address, it's a gift from a Mr Peter Andre.' Claire said she screamed! She couldn't believe it, she couldn't believe I'd done it. She's named it Daisy and her little boy loves going out for rides with her. It's a little indulgence, the least I can do after everything she has done for me over the years, and most importantly recently. A yellow Beetle is the car she always wanted – thank God it wasn't always a Ferrari – LOL!!

As much as the launch was an emotional night, it was also one of the happiest nights I've had. I proved so much to both myself and the press and it went down really well – I couldn't have asked for more. The support and love in that room was incredible. I couldn't have asked for more, there were lots of press, radio and TV stations there and it was a massive turning point and filled me with a huge amount of confidence. It had been a real challenge, and it was one I rose to. Another string to my bow, so to speak. I had given the best performance possible and your best is all anyone can ask for.

In many ways, after all these years, I am finally living my dream properly. I have always wanted to release something on my own terms, and now I have done that. It's an absolute bonus that it has had success. The support I have had I never expected and I am truly grateful for it. When I left Kate I honestly thought the public would turn against me. I was prepared for my career to end because I thought people would hate me so much for leaving, and ultimately I knew I could accept that in order to gain some peace in my life. I never expected for the support to be as it has been. I only have to pop to the petrol station and someone will shout at me, 'Keep your chin up, Pete!' It's been incredible. I don't mind admitting that I'm quite enjoying the attention. I can tell you that I'm going to enjoy this moment, every minute of it.

ON TOUR
ONCE MORE

W HO WOULD HAVE THOUGHT THAT AFTER TWENTY YEARS IN THE BUSINESS I WOULD BE OFF TOURING AGAIN? CERTAINLY NOT ME! This is the icing on the cake as far as I am concerned, and the cherry is the arena tour at the end of the year – first week sales of 10,000 tickets! How amazing is that? It was my dream fifteen years ago to perform at Wembley Arena and I did it. Now I am doing an arena tour once more – a sign of my real comeback. I love touring and performing and hope that everyone has enjoyed the shows as much as me.

The build-up to the current tour has been quite full-on and I have been rehearsing at every available opportunity. I have a studio at my house and space to practise but I needed to be physically fit too. This was a thirty-eight-date tour, so pretty tough going on the body. In the run-up I worked out every day in the gym, but I didn't concentrate on weights and building myself up, I worked on my overall fitness because you need stamina when you're on stage night after night. I'm quite happy with my body for once, although I still have hang-ups. I am never going to love the way I look, I will always be critical, I'm sure. Whether it's because I want to work on the weights and be bulkier, or whether it's the opposite and at times I think I look too bulky, there's always something I want to work on or perfect. That's just the way I am. I think that's probably quite normal. I'm not sure most people can say hand on heart, 'I love my body.'

In the recent magazine shoots that I've done I often get asked to take my top off, and although they sometimes get their way I do feel uneasy about doing it. You might not know it, but I still question the way I look. I have lost three stone since my split with Kate and I'm fitter than I've been in years, but I'm still self-conscious and no matter how many times I hear that the girls like the way I look and that I have nothing to worry about, I genuinely find it hard to believe. I have to be feeling confident on the day of a shoot to get my kit off, and I make sure I have had a good work-out beforehand! I feel happy that I seem to have my weight under control for once and I'm maintaining it by being healthy and exercising. But I don't want to be the person doing sit-ups on a plane while everyone else is getting some shut-eye again, thank you very much. This time I'll stay fit and look after myself sensibly and healthily.

'I HAVE TO BE FEELING CONFIDENT ON THE DAY OF A SHOOT TO GET MY KIT OFF, AND I MAKE SURE I HAVE HAD A GOOD WORK-OUT BEFOREHAND!'

I t was really important to me to put on a show that was bigger and better than anything I've ever done before – a tall order given that on the 'Natural' tour we had acrobats and dancers and I dropped down onto the stage in a cage! But I wanted this tour to be very different, to have a more grown-up, adult feel about it – still fun but a bit more serious. Instead of the baggy clothes I was once known for I wore slick suits and the whole feel of the show was very different to anything I'd done before, reflective of the new-style music. This was a proper production and I had input into every aspect of it; it was so exhilarating to be a part of that, and to know that it was my vision.

My inspiration has always been Michael Jackson, so I decided to approach the choreographer Sean Cheeseman. Sean choreographed several of Michael's videos, like 'Scream', 'The Way You Make Me Feel' and 'Bad', and choreographed some of Michael's tours, as well as working with Janet Jackson too. I was honoured that he agreed to work with me – without him it wouldn't have been half the show it turned out to be. I had a section which was a tribute to the Jacksons, and I wanted it to be as spot-on as possible, to make the King of Pop proud.

About a year before we moved to Los Angeles in 2009, we went for a holiday and stayed in Encino, the neighbourhood the Jacksons live in. (We stayed at an amazing house called the White House. But not the White House, obviously!) I'd met Tito Jackson and we'd swapped numbers and when I got to LA we arranged to meet up. The deal was we'd take each other out for lunch – he'd pick me up and I'd pick up the bill. He turned up in his trademark Rolls Royce bought for him by his brother Michael and has all his brothers' signatures on the roof. We were going for Japanese, and before we went to the restaurant he took me to his family's house. I couldn't believe it; I'd known what the house looked like since I was a child but to actually be there and have a look around was something else. The massive iron gates were opening for us . . . I was at Michael Jackson's family home and my jaw was on the ground in disbelief. I was in heaven! I will always thank Tito for that amazing experience. After Michael died we got closer. When I heard the news about his brother being in a coma I sent Tito a text saying, 'Please, tell me this isn't true!' He replied, 'I'm going to the hospital to find out . . .' Imagine not even knowing what's going on with your own brother? I was surprised that he managed to text me back at such a time, but he did and since then we've kept in touch and have become really good friends. Tito is a very special person to me and I feel for the Jackson family so much. For that reason I wanted to make sure that my tribute hit the right spot and was true to Michael's work.

The Jackson tribute section was also special because it was Junior's favourite part of the show. I missed the kids massively while I was on tour and travelled back home whenever I could. I can't cope not seeing my children for a long period of time and that part of touring is probably the hardest, when you are away from your creature comforts and those you love. I'd often drive through the night to get back home so that I could spend the daytimes with them. The children came to see the shows on the weekends because it was too late for them to stay up in the week. But I didn't want to deprive them from seeing it entirely, especially as Junior had become totally obsessed with my rehearsals. Because JJ is such a little showman, he came up on stage with me in rehearsals and actually he upstaged me! The crew went wild; I think he has more fans than me! I joked beforehand that instead of it being 'Peter Andre: Revelation' it would be 'Junior Andre: Revolution' and sure enough it was. I forget that people feel they almost know the kids because of the reality show and they get more attention as me these days I think. Junior loved it – I think he'd like to be on stage himself one day, although we'll discuss that nearer the time!

Just like JJ, undoubtedly my passion for music has always been apparent but the Andreas are a pretty musical family generally. On this latest tour I added a section for my brothers where we all play together on stage, which was great. Mike is a brilliant DJ and Chris came over from Australia – he can play eleven instruments! Chris is an amazing flamenco guitarist, he's incredible and the real talent of the family! My support act on tour was Laura White from *X Factor*, who was fantastic. I have always been a big fan of hers ever since she was on the show, so I was pleased when she asked to open each night. I also had the girl band GL2 to support me, so I was surrounded by lovely ladies. All in all, the tour was a huge success and the hard work, long hours and effort paid off – now I can't wait until the arena tour in December, which I know is going to be the best yet.

'I HAD A SECTION WHICH WAS A TRIBUTE TO THE JACKSONS, AND I WANTED IT TO BE AS SPOT-ON AS POSSIBLE, TO MAKE THE KING OF POP PROUD.'

As well as the tour, I have had another album out in 2010, *Unconditional Love Songs*, which went to number seven in the album charts which I was very happy with. It's a compilation of love songs I've recorded over the last fifteen years, including an incredible duet with Brian McKnight. There was a fair bit of publicity around the time of the album launch after my interview on Sky News went horribly wrong. I couldn't believe it. I'd arranged to do a lot of interviews, as you do when you are promoting an album. Then, on the same day that I was scheduled to have the interview my ex-wife got remarried overnight in Las Vegas. So guess what they wanted to talk to me about? (It was the same the last time I launched an album – Kate went on television and said I had a new girlfriend, even though I didn't, so then I got questions on that.) In the end the Sky interviewer, Kay Burley, pushed me so hard on a subject that I am so sensitive about – the children, and the idea of them being taken from me – I broke down and asked her to stop the interview. It's all a bit of a blur to me now but at the time I was extremely upset, the interviewer hit a really raw nerve. She could have asked me anything, but she brought my children into it and I got very emotional. Perhaps some people thought I was upset about Kate getting married, but that wasn't the case at all. I am genuinely pleased that she has found someone and that she is happy, but I'm still weak when it comes to the kids. I know I should ignore some of what goes on and when I react to it it makes things worse, but it's very hard. People that criticize me perhaps don't have kids themselves, otherwise they'd understand; I know most people would be just as emotional as me in the same situation.

Unconditional Love Songs came out of nowhere, really, but my fans have supported me yet again. They are truly loyal to me and I love them for that. I have done hundreds of signings all over the country for the album and I love meeting my fans – even if I'm having a bad day they cheer me up and make me smile. The passion that they seem to have for me bowls me over every time: I have to pinch myself when I think that they are here to see little old me. However many hours we have scheduled for signings I always manage to over-run, not just by a few minutes sometimes but in many cases hours – one place I stayed and signed until midnight! At one store 10,000 people turned up. I am so grateful to everyone that's come along that I try to see each and every one of them. I can't bear the idea of people queuing up for hours on end and then me not being able to speak to them. I know I cause my management headaches when I say I'm staying until I reach the end of the queue, but all my fans mean a lot to me and I don't want them leaving disappointed. I'm not stupid, I wouldn't be where I am today if it wasn't for them and I want them to know that I really am very grateful.

Aside from my music, I have a new fragrance about to hit the shelves. After the success of my perfume for women, 'Unconditional', I'm launching a men's scent, 'Conditional'. At first I came up with the idea of calling it 'Distinctive' . . . but then I thought if people didn't like it they might call it Stink! It's due out in time for Father's Day, which is very exciting, so I hope that men like the scent as much as women have! I've chosen the bottles and at present I am finalizing the scent. I know just how I want it to be. I'm quite specific about it and hands-on. All in all it's been a busy year so far, and we're not even halfway through. I've hardly had a minute to think, let alone dwell on anything – being busy is a welcome distraction and doing something that I love is a complete bonus. You never know how long it will last and in this business you can be here one day and gone the next – I know that from previous experience – so for that reason I am trying to enjoy and savour every minute.

I'M VERY PROUD OF MY FRAGRANCE FOR WOMEN, UNCONDITIONAL.

his year I've really settled in the house in Brighton, but I'm looking to buy somewhere else and put down permanent roots. At first it was strange starting out again and choosing new furniture – I'd been used to asking opinions and advice and now it was just down to me. The house was a blank canvas so I could have exactly what I wanted, and the main thing I wanted to surround myself with was the kids. Going from seeing them every day to far less frequently I wanted to have their presence near me all of the time, so I had huge canvases made of each one of them. You can see them in this book. One in the living room is a picture of me linking hands with Harvey, Tiaamii and Junior. Our backs are to the camera, our feet are all in sync and we're dressed in denim dungarees. I love it. It was taken on a shoot for *OK!* magazine, just outside Palm Springs. It was quite an experience because the location was a trailer park in the middle of nowhere and some of the characters we met were quite, how shall we say . . . different?! Looking back, it was very funny. One guy came up to us with his dog. It looked quite cute, but I was worried about the kids because they have no fear at all around dogs and I didn't really know if it was as friendly as it looked. We decided to ask the guy if he would mind being in the pictures but first he had to sign a release form to agree to his image being used. That was a bit of a problem – he told us he couldn't sign the form because he was on the run! Suddenly the dog seemed all the more scary and I started to think, 'Where the hell are we?' Over the years we have had some really beautiful pictures taken for shoots we've done, and another one I particularly like is a brilliant shot of my feet, Kate's feet and Tiaamii's feet hanging out of the end of the duvet. It's great!

The Brighton house is gorgeous: you can see it on *Going It Alone*. It has everything I need. There's a swimming pool in the back garden, which the kids love, as well as a barbecue for sunny days – any excuse for a barbie picnic! The children have two homes now, and I want them to feel comfortable so there's a playroom full of their toys downstairs and I've had beds made for each of their rooms with their names carved into them. I like the fact that I'm away from London and can get some peace and quiet. Having said that, the fans do know where we live and often camp outside waiting for us. They will leave food or cakes on the doorstep to fatten me up! It's sweet, really, although if and when I move it might have to be to a house up a long driveway because the other day some overexcited fans broke my gates! In Brighton it's not as private as I'd like ideally and I think that a bit of privacy at times is important. I have shared a lot of my life with the public and it's been great, but I do still want some 'me' time.

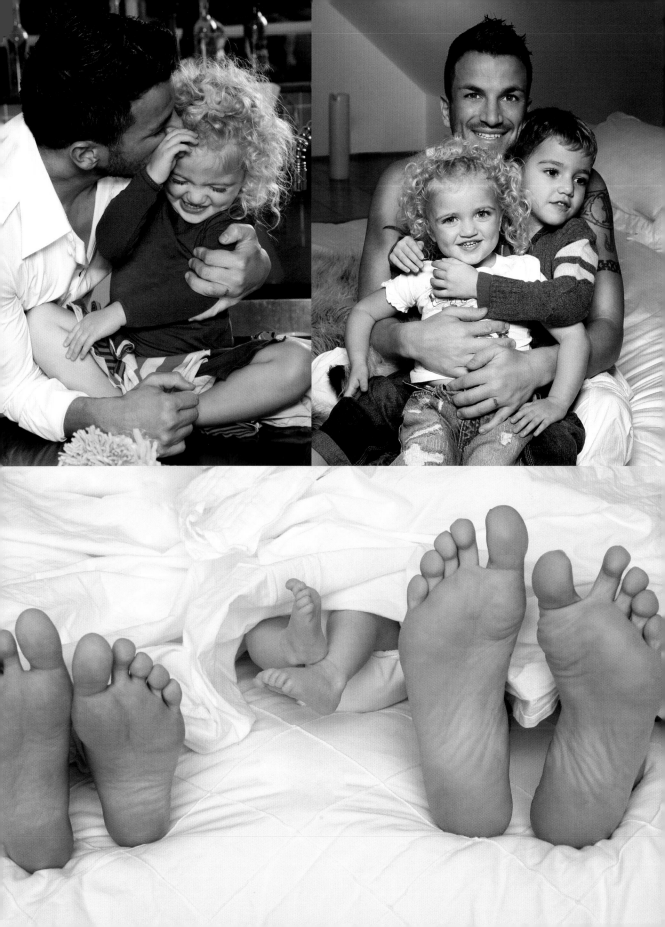

Some of the best experiences I have these days are spent with the children, quality time, just me and them. I had loads of great holidays with the kids last year. We spent a week in Marbella – it was partly work-related as I was doing a shoot there but we got to spend loads of quality time together in the warmth. Having been in a warm climate for most of my life, I crave that sort of weather and Marbella was perfect. The house we stayed in was beautiful and the kids got to swim every day and do everything they love to do. We had dinner at Jean-Christophe Novelli's restaurant which was fantastic and one evening they even came to the villa and cooked for us. Nicola McLean, her husband Tom and their son Rocky also joined us while we were there and we became great friends. As well as Marbella, last October I took all three kids to Center Parcs for a long weekend break – we had an ace time and it was so nice to get away from it all. It's a great place for children and we went to all the activities

that were going on – bike-rides, painting, walks in the woods, we even managed to fit in a game of pool! Junior in particular loved all the different activities like painting egg-cups and mugs, but we did everything together, as a family. It was lovely spending so much time with the kids one-on-one. This year we've been to Dubai and in the summer we're due to go to visit the family in Australia, just me and the kids, which will be fantastic. I'm really looking forward to it. These holidays do wonders for us as a family. Junior and I have always had a close bond whereas Tiaamii used to be much more of a mummy's girl, but the more time we've spent together in the past year the closer we have become. It's got to the point now where she makes me stay with her when I put her to bed. She doesn't like me to be out of her sight and will say to me, 'Daddy, don't go! Another story, Daddy!' Of course, she only needs to look at me with those big blue eyes and I give in and stay with her until she falls asleep.

'HAVING BEEN IN A WARM CLIMATE FOR MOST OF MY LIFE, I CRAVE THAT SORT OF WEATHER AND MARBELLA WAS PERFECT.'

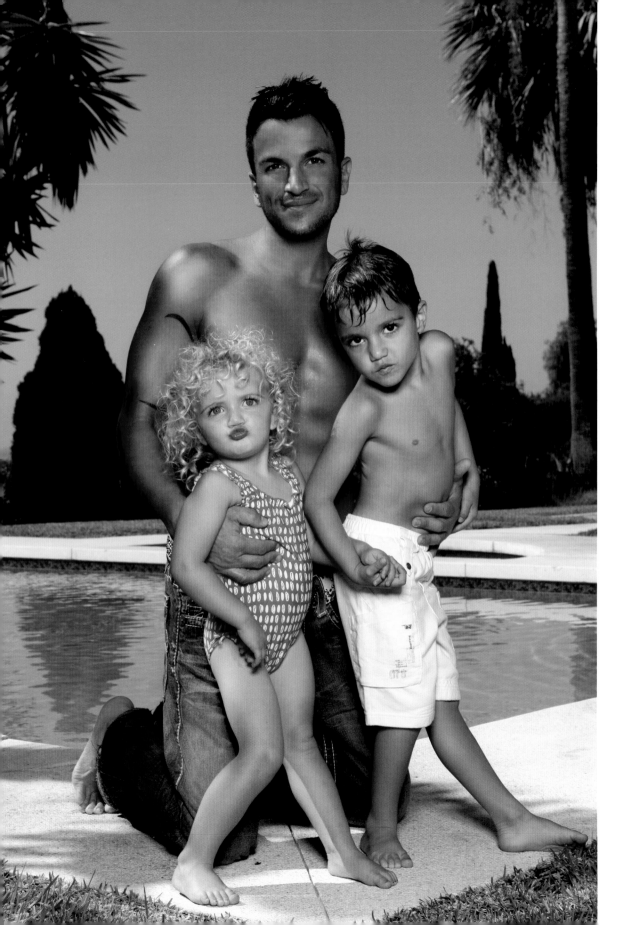

I TOOK ALL THREE KIDS
TO CENTER PARCS FOR
A LONG WEEKEND BREAK.
WE HAD AN ACE TIME AND
IT WAS SO NICE TO GET
AWAY FROM IT ALL. JUNIOR
IN PARTICULAR LOVED ALL
THE DIFFERENT ACTIVITIES
SUCH AS PAINTING EGG-
CUPS AND MUGS

These days I don't have a nanny to help out with the children, I prefer to spend time with them and look after them myself, apart from when I'm at work and I have my cousin Miranda and her husband Pete come and look after them at home for me. They are so loved by the kids and me, so it's great having them around. When Harvey comes to stay he does have a nanny. He has quite specialist needs and must be looked after all the time, but although he needs continual care and has to be watched closely he is such a good lad. But like with all children, you have to keep your eye on them. To not have a nanny for Junior and Tiaamii was a decision I made a few months ago, and so far it's worked out really well and I've not regretted it. They're such good kids and I don't get enough time with them as it is because I have to work, so when I do have them I want to be with them one hundred per cent of the time. Getting them up in the mornings, making their breakfast, getting them dressed, cooking their tea, putting them to bed – I want to be a part of it all and not miss out on a thing.

I'm feeling more comfortable and happy now in myself and my ability to look after the kids, run a home and generally conduct an adult life! I expect a lot of people think I have a wild celebrity lifestyle, where I throw parties all the time, but in reality I'm afraid to say it's a lot less interesting. Behind closed doors I am actually a pretty normal and regular guy. I love to do things that everyone else loves to do. Don't get me wrong, I do love to throw parties at the house occasionally, but never when kids are there. Mostly, if I'm not working, I love the chance to have an early night. The glamour stops when I get back from work, whether that's rehearsals or a launch or a signing, and I'm often tucked up in my huge eight-foot bed by 10 p.m. When the kids are at home, they'll ask if they can stay in with me and we'll climb in and watch a film together – it's bliss. I'd choose that over everything. You see, it isn't that exciting chez Andre!

Aside from going to bed early, I also enjoy cooking – it's actually a bit of a hobby for me and I really love it. Living with Mike is great because we've both always loved our food. He shops and I cook. We often cook meals together and have people around to the house, and of course we have lots of barbecues. I'll try to experiment with a new dish, pasta being my favourite. It's important that the children get to eat fresh food and so I always try to cook up a treat when they are over. I even tried my hand at baking cupcakes last Valentine's Day for Tiaamii – the kitchen was a mess! That week I stood in for Philip Schofield to present *This Morning*. Because it was Valentine's week there were loads of heart-shaped balloons at the back of the studio. Cheekily, I asked if I could take some home for Tiaamii, Junior and Harvey who were staying with me that weekend. They loved them. As a single father I've become pretty domesticated and I'm embracing it. I am learning new things every day – I can only get better, I hope. I like to hang out with my mate Ryan now I'm single again, he comes over and we watch movies and chill out. On the occasions I do go out with the lads it still feels quite strange, because while I was married that sort of thing wasn't a part of my life. Kate didn't like me to socialize with the boys, so I didn't and now getting back out on the scene is quite a strange feeling. But I am my own man again now, free to come and go as I please and that is weird. I need to get used to it! I'm sure that I will eventually. It's quite difficult to plan much at the moment because the year ahead is so busy – it's already been jam-packed with work. But I'm not complaining, I'd rather have too much than too little! Fortunately the craziness shows no sign of stopping just yet and that's fine by me.

SO, WHAT DOES THE FUTURE HOLD?

LOOKING BACK OVER MY LIFE SO FAR, I CAN SEE HOW LUCKY I'VE BEEN. FINANCIALLY I'M SECURE, AND THE KIDS WON'T HAVE TO WORRY ABOUT THEIR FUTURE. My dad always invested my earnings for me: for a long time I didn't get to see any of the money I earned. I was known from such a young age that if I had got my hands on the cash at the time I'd have wanted to spend it. Instead, my father invested money in a property portfolio for me and I've always had that for a rainy day. I have a house in Cyprus, houses in Australia and property here – myself and my children will be looked after. Even if everything had gone belly-up I would have had something left – Dad has always been a good businessman and I'm very grateful to him. When people say that I went into the jungle with nothing, that it was my appearance on *I'm A Celebrity. . .* and my relationship with Kate that made me money again, it makes me laugh. That really wasn't the case. Dad's investments have stood me in good stead, and I've been able to have some say in what I do rather than having to say yes to everything that comes along.

But I'm not about to sit at home and rest on my laurels. I am ambitious and want to try new things, set myself new challenges. My management are a help, pushing me but also helping me know my limitations. I'm definitely not ready to retire. My new series has just started and I've had a great crew to work with – it's like one big happy family and we have a lot of laughs together.

I've been thinking about the future, and in a perfect world I'd prefer my kids not to go into the world of the media and celebrity – I wouldn't encourage them and I wouldn't discourage them, but it wouldn't be my ideal scenario for any of them. I have lived it, and you need to be a very strong character to survive. I know it sounds contradictory because it has been my living since such an early age, but I don't want to have to see my kids go through some of the pain I have been through, no parent wants to see that. I expect the life that they have been born into will mean that they go one way or the other, they will either love it or hate it and I won't be able to stand in judgement, I know that! (Of course, Tiaamii is going to be nun, okay!) Even though my career is going really well at the moment, I would love to spend more time in Australia. But because my children are here, I'm here – it will always be that way. Wherever they are, I will be. If I'm going to be here and the kids are here, I want to have a regular gig, a secure job that provides for us and that I enjoy. It's stability I'd like: to know I can go to work and then come home in the evening. I've thought about it long and hard and I think that job is in television.

Already, I have my slot on *This Morning*, which I love. Some weeks I get to guest-present too, which is brilliant. On those occasions it has been quite daunting – I thoroughly enjoy it but it's nerve-racking because it's live so there is no room for error! I think if I'm totally true to myself I prefer doing pre-recordings at the moment, but I'm grateful that I am being given these opportunities and that TV companies are putting their faith in me. I often cover the red carpet events and interview the stars behind the scenes, which is exciting – it's a role reversal! In February I presented The Brits backstage. I had a bit of a spray tan just before the show . . . I couldn't resist. When you're around all these stars looking lovely and brown you feel a bit pasty, so I wanted in on the action! I'd far prefer a natural tan but even Mike, who was with me, got envious and had a light spray. Then Claire got in on the action, then everyone wanted to be as brown. We all looked like we'd been on holiday in the sun for a month!

Being backstage I had the best seat in the house and got to meet all of the big acts. In particular, a highlight of the night had to be meeting Dame Shirley Bassey. It was an honour, it was like meeting Elvis – she is such a genius. While I was there I became a huge (and admittedly late) fan of Kasabian. I watched Tom, the lead singer, and the band rehearsing and couldn't believe how he just stood there, so focused, singing with all the madness going on around him. He was an absolute professional and I really admire him for that. I kept bumping into JLS – they are really nice guys and deserve their success. I like how down to earth they are and unaffected, it's nice to see. Dizzee Rascal came over for a chat – what a legend! He really made me laugh because in the ten minutes we were talking he managed to say thirteen f*cks and two sh*ts! I also had a chat with Liam Gallagher – some people might be surprised to know that we exchanged a few words about family and kids. Seriously! And how could I forget the stunning Alicia Keys, who hung out in my dressing room for a while. Amazing.

I also got to speak to the very gorgeous Cheryl Cole. I didn't ask her anything personal, I wanted to know about her performance and she was lovely. There is a weird dynamic, I think, when I interview other celebs because they don't see me posing the same threat as a journalist and that's really nice, so often I get a lot of access because they know I'm not about to grill them! I interviewed Robbie Williams while I was there, which was an absolute pleasure. He was such a nice guy, we chatted for about half an hour and he seemed really happy and settled. I have a massive amount of respect for Robbie. He's sold fifty-seven million albums – how huge is that? (When I was chatting to him I got it wrong and said fifty-five million albums and he corrected me. But hey, what's a couple of million between mates?) With Robbie, like with many of these huge celebrities, when I think I am interviewing them and chatting away with them, I feel humbled, it's weird. I love music but I am really enjoying this new career path too.

I worked over three days so I could interview everyone and I almost did it – it was only Lady Gaga who I didn't speak to. She wanted to be interviewed but on the night she was too upset after the death of Alexander McQueen. Backstage there didn't seem to be any big egos, just people trying to get on with the job in hand. Yes, there was the craziness of Gaga – her performance, her outfit, her entourage – but it was like one big family, a beautiful atmosphere and I loved every minute of it. I had my brother with me and we had some experiences I will never forget, just as we did at the MOBOs backstage last year, and I loved that too. These musicians are all so talented and the experiences and opportunities that I'm being given I'm determined to grasp, enjoy and learn from. I am very lucky to be in this position, and professionally I'm loving that aspect of life.

ABOVE: BACKSTAGE AT THE
BRITS — IT WAS BRILLIANT FUN
INTERVIEWING ALL THESE AMAZING
MUSICIANS.

LEFT: PETER AND HIS ROAD
MANAGER CARL MACHIN

Personally, I think I've finally turned a corner in these last few months. Like in any split there have been a lot of ups and downs and privately some very hard times. That's the truth and I'm sure that anyone going through something similar would say the same thing. Life is turned upside down: you are used to seeing the kids every day and suddenly you can't; you're used to living in a house with all your belongings around you and suddenly you're not. It's a shock to the system. Now I have built up a barrier and not a lot gets through it any more. I've made a conscious effort to stop looking at the papers every day and that is a great help. Seeing the gossip written in the papers and magazines doesn't help the moving-on process – I go forward ten steps and then see something that upsets me and go back twenty paces. So if I don't look, it can't hurt, can it? At some point I will have to move-on fully and although I'm pretty much there, my wounds haven't entirely healed. Even up until a few months ago I was still very down about what had happened. My appetite hadn't fully come back and I felt sick about it all. These days, though, it's very different and I am surprised by my own reaction. Things don't shock me any more, in the way that they would have done a few months back. It's acceptance of the situation, I guess. You are hurt, you have the tears, then you have the anger, then you have that resolute feeling. You see so much you become numb to it all. A lot of crap has been thrown, some has stuck but most of it has made me stronger and has taught me to deal with the worst someone can do to you. On the whole the media has been great to me (give or take a few reviews!) and I understand that they have a job to do. I also understand that not everyone is going to like me, sadly, or that that they could like me one minute and then not the next – fame's a fickle industry that chews people up and spits them out when they are done. If I do have any magazines or newspapers in the house I keep them away from the kids as I don't want them confused.

'PERSONALLY, I THINK I'VE FINALLY TURNED A CORNER IN THESE LAST FEW MONTHS. LIKE IN ANY SPLIT THERE HAVE BEEN A LOT OF UPS AND DOWNS AND PRIVATELY SOME VERY HARD TIMES.'

For my children's sake I try to be strong, and I am very careful to try to make sure that they will always be proud of me, but I'm not an angel and I won't always do the right thing. I don't want them to ever read something that I've said or done that will hurt or upset them. The internet is available to everyone and everything is permanently documented now – my niece used to be obsessed with watching Kate and I on YouTube and I have no doubt that when our children get older they will have a look too. I try to make the right call wherever I can. I don't like it when things that should remain confidential are spilled across the papers. I can't control what others do but I want everyone to see that I had the respect and decency not to lay everything bare, that some things really are too private to share. The kids should be the focus for both Kate and I, not trying to hurt one another. I would never say anything negative about their mum to them. They are our blood and that would be wrong. It's hard enough for them as it is without feeling confused. I guess parents that have split up always feel some guilt towards their children.

I suppose I will always worry that I've failed in some way because my marriage didn't work out the way I'd hoped. With my parents reaching fifty-five years of marriage to date, I had a hard act to live up to. To my brothers and sister and me, my parents are our rock and for their fiftieth wedding anniversary we wanted them to have a massive party in Cyprus to celebrate. At the time my house in Cyprus was still being built so we held it at the Four Seasons hotel. It was the first time in years that we were all together and we partied well into the night. Even after Mum and Dad had gone to bed the rest of us carried on, until about five o'clock in the morning! A lot of friends and family had come over from Australia so we had a lot of catching up to do! For a long time it made me feel sick to think that my marriage didn't last long enough to celebrate like that – it should have been for life but it wasn't. But hurt is something that subsides and any hurt that I still have is no longer because of Katie. I want her to be happy, I have no malice in me in that respect.

On my birthday this year, 27 February 2010, I turned thirty-seven and can you believe it, I lost my voice?! I spent the whole day in bed trying to get better because I was on my 'Revelation' tour and I had to perform that night, knowing that the show must go on. I was in Edinburgh, staying in an incredible hotel that's like a castle, Prestonfield House, but I wasn't really able to enjoy it as I had bad flu and I felt ropey. No one was going to accept that though – they wanted me to have a good night no matter what. As a complete surprise Claire had travelled up, the band had made me a cake and they had all organized a meal for me after the show! I was very well looked after and received some great presents – Mike bought me the new iPad, my mate Carl, knowing how much I love Scotch, bought me some nice whisky and Claire gave me some D&G clothes. I was thoroughly spoilt, which did make me feel much better.

As well as my good friends around me, the public support has been incredible this year and I can only thank them for helping me through this. When you make such a massive decision like I did – to walk out on a relationship that was so public and would be written about day in, day out – you just don't know how people will react. The public could have turned against me; they could have disliked me or judged me for my decision. I really didn't know how people would feel about it. But, in many ways, the reality shows that we did together helped me in that respect. People had been watching and made their own minds up. I knew things weren't right but when you're in the thick of it you don't see it quite as clearly as somebody on the outside. On internet forums and in the papers, there was a lot of talk about our relationship, about the way things were between Katie and me. The thing is with reality TV programmes and fly-on-the-wall-style documentaries, they can't really lie, you get to see quite literally what is going on behind closed doors. I understand that people want to know what happened – they feel as though they have watched our relationship grow from the very beginning but what's happened has been and gone and now I need to look to the future.

It's a new century and a new me. When Kate got remarried I knew that the time was right to remove the tattoo on my wedding finger. I originally kept it because I didn't want to confuse the children, but the time came to get rid of it. I haven't wanted it there for a long while but I didn't want to upset the kids or make any more changes than were absolutely necessary. Now their mum has got remarried it seems okay to do it – the perfect and final cut-off. We have both moved on.

I am really looking forward to the next step and embarking on a new relationship: although I am still very nervous, and it will be hard to trust again, I've started looking. I'm not a monk but I don't want to tell the press everything. What I do know is that next time round, I'll do things very differently. A lot of lessons have been learned but I'd like to think that I'll meet someone who will be the perfect person for me to settle down with. I'm a family man and I crave that again. I'm not getting any younger and I know that I would love to have more children at some point, if I am lucky enough. When the kids are here the house is so busy with fun and laughter and I love every minute, so when they leave to go back to their mum it feels very empty and it's painfully hard. Work is really busy, and takes my mind off it for a bit, but there is still that horrible emptiness when the children are gone. To have to say goodbye to them when it's time for them to go back is so difficult. No father wants to be away from their children. In this case there is no other alternative, but that doesn't help. The kids are probably the only way I can be hurt any more, and saying goodbye each week doesn't get any easier with time. Next time round, I'd like to be with someone who feels that family is enough and their priority is the home life . . . maybe a nice Greek or Italian lady, an 'English Rose', or even my biggest attraction, someone from the Caribbean. Whoever I'm with, one thing is for sure – now that I'm back on the dating scene I want to make sure that I don't flaunt it. The children won't be involved unless that person is announced as my girlfriend – I don't want to confuse them, so they will be introduced as just a friend first. When the time comes they will be introduced slowly: the kids need to like them and feel comfortable around them. Ultimately, my children need stability and I will give them that in spades. One of my biggest concerns is that whatever mistakes I make, I don't make them in front of my children. To this day, to this moment, I have never been intimate with anyone in front of my children, except their mother. And as I say, I better be damn sure about that someone before it happens. I'll leave it here . . . after all, who knows what will happen in the future. All I know now is that I have three beautiful kids in my life out of my marriage to Katie, and for that reason I will never regret the past.

There's an old saying that mothers tell their daughters, that you have to kiss a few frogs before you meet your prince. I don't know what the equivalent saying is for guys – although I know that I'm not planning on heading down to the nearest pond to start looking for frogs... That probably sounds terrible, but I guess what I mean is that although I'm going to date carefully, I know that true love doesn't just land in your lap and I may not find my princess straight away. If the past has taught me anything it's that the important thing in both life and love is to know what you're looking for and to not give up trying to find it. This year is probably one of the biggest I've ever had: it's going to be a good year, I just know it. Of course there will be ups and downs, but at the moment I feel very happy and blessed. A chapter of my life has finally closed and the old saying 'What doesn't kill you makes you stronger' has proved very true. For someone not yet forty years old, I have been lucky enough to experience more than some people do in a lifetime. I hope from reading this book that you can see that with me, what you see is what you get. Claire says I make it 'Cool to be Nice', which is a lovely thing to say and I hope she's right. I really appreciate you – the public – supporting me through those bad times. Because I'm bound to make more mistakes! I still do silly things. I'm not a saint – I'm a man. And I'm trying to be a good man. I'm doing the best I can. As I write this I can honestly declare that the old Peter Andre is back – this time a new, improved and wiser version!

'I FEEL VERY HAPPY AND BLESSED. A CHAPTER OF MY LIFE HAS FINALLY CLOSED AND THE OLD SAYING 'WHAT DOESN'T KILL YOU MAKES YOU STRONGER' HAS PROVED VERY TRUE. FOR SOMEONE NOT YET FORTY YEARS OLD, I HAVE BEEN LUCKY ENOUGH TO EXPERIENCE MORE THAN SOME PEOPLE DO IN A LIFETIME.'

ACKNOWLEDGEMENTS

Thank you first of all to my three beautiful children, Junior, Tiaamii and Harvey: you are my world. To my mum, Thea, and my dad, Savva: thank you for always being there for me. To all my brothers — Andrew, Chris, Danny and Michael — and to my sister, Debbie: your strength and support over the last year has been invaluable. (Special thanks to Mike, who has been with me every step of the way — I owe you bro.) Thanks also to my niece and nephew, Thea and Savandy, and to my close friends Rene Nicastro, George Nicolaou, Nick Baker and Ryan Jackson.

To my management team, Can Associates, who have guided me and made sure I saw the light at the end of the tunnel, a heartfelt thank you. They too have been to hell and back, and their loyalty will never be forgotten. Claire, Neville and Nicola — you're the best.

Thanks to Hannah Fernando, my friend, who has helped me complete this book. Talking about many of these things isn't easy and you've helped me find the words. And to everyone at Penguin, who have allowed me to indulge in all of my past experiences, good and bad! I've enjoyed every minute, and I hope readers will enjoy the journey too.

To the media: I asked you into my life and through the years you've given me my fair share of criticism, but you have also supported me and for that I thank you.

And, of course, finally, thanks to the Great British Public, and my fans in particular, for your invaluable support. Thank you so much for giving me my life back.

x x x